Soul External

Rediscovering the Great Blue Heron

story by

Steven H. Semken

Illustrations
&
typographic layout

Andrew R. Driscoll

Soul External: Rediscovering the Great Blue Heron

Copyright © 2015 Steven H. Semken
Illustrations © 2015 Andrew R. Driscoll

ISBN 9781888160628

Library of Congress Control Number: 2010921466

Ice Cube Press, LLC (Est. 1993)
205 N. Front Street North Liberty, Iowa 52317
www.icecubepress.com
steve@icecubepress.com
twitter: @icecubepress

Andrew R. Driscoll
may be reached via:
Desiderat.AD@gmail.com
creative work viewable at:
AndrewRDriscoll@wordpress.com

'yellow spiral' proof print by John Talleur,
Eurydice Unbound, 1988.
collection Andrew R. Driscoll

First Edition

This book previously appeared in different format and content
as *The Great Blues*, Woodley Press, ISBN 9780939391363, ©2005.
This version of the book was awarded a Kansas Notable Book Award in 2006.
The chapter "The Flavor of Brass" appeared in different form in *Wakarusa
Wetlands: In Word & Image* ©2005 Lawrence Committee on Imagination
and Place, Lawrence Art Center

to Laura Lee & Fenna Marie
two flying beauties
full of immaculate soul

≈

for
K & P
personifications
of the very deep truth
—that interior
image

At length dame Venus sawe her sonne obteyne the upper hand.

King Turnus fell, and eeke the towne of Ardea wich did stand

Ryght strong in hygh estate as long as Turnus lived. But

Assonone as that Aennaeas swoord to death had Turnus put,

The towne was set on fyre: and from amid the embers flew

A fowle which till that present tyme no persone ever knew,

And beete the ashes feercely up with flapping of his wing.

The leanenesse, palenesse, dolefull sound, and every other thing

That may expresse a Citie sakt, yea and the cities name

Remayned still unto the bird. And now the verrye same

With Hernesewes fethers dooth bewayle the towne,
                                        wherof it came.

Ovid.

"To those devoid of imagination
a blank place on the map is useless waste;
to others, the most useful part."

Aldo Leopold.

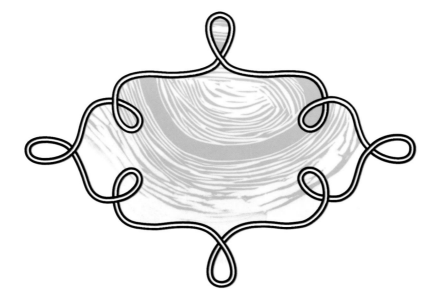

"Reassured by our indifference
other creatures may come
calling, asking
who we are, ready to visit."

Gary Holthaus.

FIRST HINT

The only thing necessary was a shard of evidence. I just needed some tiny hint or clue to reveal what was happening, needed something turned in my imaginary favor to tilt and better explain the magical amalgam so coiled in my head as I sat gawking and marveling during my first excursion to a rookery of great blue herons. I wanted some proof that the birds and their habitat were real.

Following the rough directions given to me from a friend, I journeyed to a spot so obscured, well concealed and safe I trembled with the feeling of immensity. The directions involved a faint line drawing on the back side of a deposit slip. I was told to follow a series of gravel roads until I reached a "NO TRESPASSING" sign. Finally, I was instructed, "If anyone asks what you're doing, just tell them you're with the Kansas Bird and Game Division." No one ever asked. Over the years the journey to the rookery took on many meanings, parking in front of the no trespassing sign I even convinced myself I was with the Kansas Bird and Game Division. I slowly turned this journey to the herons into a ritual, it was a calling, a pilgrimage. But, on this first trip to the rookery my grips on sanity and reality were erased. When I arrived at the heart of the rookery, I became frazzled and lost as above me drifted ninety, perhaps more than a hundred great blue herons.

The herons were so close I could hear their wings flap, see the raspy vibrations of feathers ruffling in flight, noticed how they rocked gently up and down in the air with each flap of their wings. When I first arrived maybe fifty of them rose and drifted in different directions, then slowly, ever so slowly, each relaxed in my presence, resettling on their nests. At one time or another there were at least fifteen or so of the birds rising, flying, coming to and from a nest.

As I watched in awe, fully enraptured, these tall birds were engaged in a multitude of activities. Some were perched on the limbs of the ghostly, tall, old-growth sycamore trees. Others landed on the earth beside a narrow woodland creek to stare, heads slightly tilted in odd angles, at the slowly moving creek water, whilst others circled wide and high overhead. Watching them so intently my eyes were busy darting back and forth and I am convinced I hypnotized myself. I do know I began whispering semi-nonsense under
my breath
        …amazing, wow, holy crap, my God….
                                   no doubt
time absolutely stood still. I couldn't believe it when a couple of the birds began puffing out their long, plume feathers and then, in further amazement, I observed each of them wrap their wings around themselves as though dressing in robes. I was so enamored, so intrigued it wouldn't have surprised me if I had looked up and noticed a colony of herons hanging upside down in the trees like giant bats. As the crescendo of activity caused from my initial arrival wore off, I observed the males offering their female companions sticks to build nests.

I noticed the small heads of fledgling herons peaking just above the rim of nests, and then, lightly, I made out the slightest peeps of these babies calling for food. Such hospitality and trust before me. I wondered if I had been invited, or was intruding. Either way my blood was rushing and my mind had taken on an irrational way of thinking. Gravity was gushing at all directions and I had never felt more alive, more mystic, more spiritual, more engaged in the world at one moment. I was amazed, illuminated, and frightened with immensity all at once. There was no question at that moment I had truly found the center of the world, right here in an isolated corner of northeastern Kansas.

As Mircea Eliade said,

"the discovery or projection of a fixed point

— the center —

is equivalent to the creation of the world."

Honestly, I felt I had discovered a charmed, and perfect world. That this spot would become the center of my world was no more, no less than completely obvious.

These great blue birds and their hermetic habits merge with all my preconceived notions regarding dreams and reality—hopes and fears. No clear detail stands out as the cause for my sudden infatuation. Perhaps it was the odor of wild mushrooms and guano in the air, or the piles of pale white bone strewn on the ground amongst the leaves and branches of the sycamore trees hosting the herons' nests. Perhaps it was the eerie variety of noises: *clacking, squalling,* and *barking* I could distinguish coming out of the herons' long curvy necks? I do remember chuckling at myself, remembering I had believed the great blue heron unable to make more than one strained utterance. I observed and listened intensely, breathing heavily, taking in odors as best my human senses could. There were clearly as many as fourteen variety of heron noises being *sung, clucked, bellowed, whistled,* even *moaned* around me.

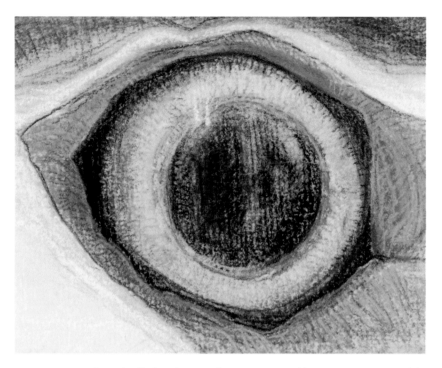

I wondered if the herons' peering yellow eyes were able to gaze straight deep into me? Could they take a voyage inside my deepest thoughts? I wondered, did the herons have any awe, any wonder toward me? Maybe it was an ironic comedy, I was at once having an epiphany over them while they were oblivious and entirely uninterested in me. Ultimately this didn't matter of course, I could behave spiritually all I wanted even if my thoughts for the herons, the creek, the trees were not exchanged. Perhaps the birds knew I would be too scared to enter a full and wild immersion, too uncomfortable to feel the texture of their feathers if any of them were to land next to me without warning, knew that I would scream and my heart would drop to my ankles if one of them quickly locked its gaze upon me. Maybe they were aware that if they stuck out their long necks and released a loud bark, I would step back, if they kept barking at me, I would slowly retreat, ashamed and even frightened, never to return. All the same, torn between *fantasy, magic, myth, reality, dreams, wonder, & hope,*

I desperately wanted to touch these semi-reptilian birds. I truly wished to smell their breath and feel the draft of air coming from the flapping of their wings.

A craving stirred in my stomach—it was obvious that some elemental, alchemical combination was being presented for me to understand. I thought of a passage in Richard Nelson's book *The Island Within* when he retells the formula for a good hunter:

"A good hunter ... that's somebody the animals come to."

This comment made me think:

What makes a good bird watcher?
Easy, someone the birds let see them.
Why, I wondered, were the great blue herons of Kansas offering themselves to me? What had I done to get so close to these creatures? I was standing right beside their nests; they were letting me watch their mating rituals and yet they seemed unashamed before me. I felt certain I was being offered a wildly crazed, prehistoric blessing.

A blessing that would soon begin to confound me. I believed I had received this approval, this stroke of luck only

if I were to journey precisely and if I were fully engaged in both my movements and thoughts. When I began to return regularly and would embark at the beginning of the trail to the rookery I felt obliged to start at the same spot each time. I would be sure to pass by the same trees, smell the same odors, touch the same large cottonwoods, sycamores, cross the creek at the exact same spot as though the area had a hold on me, was watching me. Did the tree trunks have eyes and ears? I was quite certain the birds, the creek, the plants had ways to interpret that I was proceeding correctly. I had convinced myself there must be a living, breathing, keyhole which I had to pass through in order to properly open the rookery.

Perhaps it was a magic expectation, a maze of sorts and if I did perform just the right ritualized order of actions then the land and place around me would reveal the herons. A form of simple magic, as is science, a mere cause and effect. My pausing to stare at the creek water, inhaling the odor of spring flowers, eating winter snow and embracing the soft crackly bark of the sycamore trunks melded together the local senses into me and me into the place.

I lost track of sensibility when I reached the herons.

Having gawked at their behaviors, I had the impression I was slowly sinking into the earth and more connected with this place in Kansas than I had ever felt connected with anything before. After I left this rookery for the first time, I was simply crazed with all things heron. People questioned my extreme attraction to this mysterious, winged creature and its environ. Some were even embarrassed at my diligence. I watched for hours the movement of herons along the Kaw River—trying to decipher their behavior in the morning versus their behavior in the evening; did they face the sun in the morning, or evening, how did their shadows cast;

how did shadows help with gathering food, not help; the observations were endless. I rushed to the shoreline with plaster of Paris to make molds of their footprints. I scooped up the sand they had walked in and sniffed it, a few times, late in the evening, hoping to merge with sunset's long shadows, I learned how to cast my shadow so as to appear as a heron on the surface of the land. I even rubbed their droppings on my chest and tried to imitate the half bark-half belching noise they made when startled and lifted away in flight,

Over the next fourteen years I remained stumped, trying to figure out how to explore and come to terms with these great blues and this spot on earth, this spot which I knew to be the center of the world. I never questioned my need to examine and explore this idea. I did not feel that I was being religious, but I was cherishing this place as sacred.
As Mircea Eliade wrote,
"the sacred is equivalent to a power... saturated with being."
I wanted to part the veil of this sacred power
in as full a way as I was capable.

Over time though I feared my thoughts were becoming too frenetic, too far-fetched, too beyond control. All my searching and wondering I hoped would not drive me into disarray. Abstraction and too much thinking I knew might lead to an oblique and deeply-cratered fantasy until I would be unable to tell anyone much more than a mumbling, jumble of eclectic, philosophical, psycho-spiritual hogwash. All the same, I was beginning to believe in new ways of knowing, and there was no question that theses deep woods held some supernatural, well-aged serum of truth to which I had been given access. I knew it was strange, but mixing creek water with heron feathers and sycamore seed balls was a definite tonic of truth which I enjoyed sipping. I had begun to gulp down this concoction as though an endorsement of contagious, place-based, sympathetic magic. Magic in all ways began to surround me, all beautiful and complex. If I could just learn more, pay better attention I could increase my understanding of this place. I was in the realms of both con-tagious and sympathetic forms of magic. Each rolled and swirled in my mind, at once I felt one more than the other, then back again as I tiptoed through the land, tasting creek water, observing the flight of clouds and the shapes of the herons' wings.

G. K. Chesterton commented:

"one group of people thinks that it is the wind that moves the trees; the other group thinks that the motion of the trees creates the wind"

I was unsure of up and down, myth,
or magic,
the real and the imagined.

I can't lie though. At times my wife did not understand my strains and consternations. She told me, quite matter-of-factly, I was absolutely making things too hard, "*After all,*" she declared, "*aren't you just writing about a bunch of birds in the woods?*" Aghast at the suggestion that my obsessions were trivial, I quickly pointed out that a "*bunch*" of great blue herons should properly be referred to as a *"siege"* of herons. My comment merely served my own intentions as I was the only one who knew this tidbit of knowledge. I intended my remark to demonstrate the difficult and beseeching conflicts so obviously placed before me. It was clear that my wife (*and friends*) did not entirely understand my struggles. I was certain though, given enough time, I would stumble upon, figure out, or at least come to terms with this rookery and the ever-tightening clench the twigs, feathers and trees— the herons' ways and habitat had taken hold of my mind.

What I hoped would happen is my searching would allow me to discover some never-known, but far reaching detail of the natural world. I was convinced I had entered a realm of pure discovery and was at the core of some long misunderstood and forgotten myth. Rousseau once wrote,

"It is on the summits of mountains, in the depths of the forest, or desert islands that nature reveals her most potent charms,"

with which I whole-heartedly agree.
In my opinion, I had been placed under a potent charm.
I needed only to learn to observe and decipher.

Then, about a year ago, visiting the rookery for the umpteenth time, it crossed my mind that maybe my wife was right. This was just a story about some birds, in some trees, along a creek edged with old growth cottonwood and sycamore trees. This thought allowed my problems in understanding this rookery to be mine, not the herons', not the trees', not the water's. I was close to believing this simple thought, but even as I became more comfortable, there seemed to be some sort of a blind spot forming in my upper cortex, some hitch, some stubborn belief attached to my very nerve endings which would not budge and continued to nag on the edges of my possible certainty. I was positive there was one crucial detail being overlooked and I hit upon the clue I needed in a short verse of poetry by W. S. Merwin:

"I want to tell what the forests
were like
I will have to speak
in a forgotten language."

After reading these words, a vague and seldom-utilized portion of my instinctual brain began ticking. A subtle change whirled through my lungs and sternum, moved back outside my mouth then spread across the expansive space of woodland and then further out on to the prairie nearby. I thought of how the land brings birth to all things. Of course, I thought, of course, I repeated, of course there was a truth older than words being spoken by these herons that I needed to understand. I blushed with rapture; my whole body heaved as if full of warm air.

Doug Thorpe wrote of the wild,

"a path so familiar that we don't always realize that there might be alternative routes through this wilderness."

The simple things become a piece of a larger puzzle.
I had once read about the human brain being three layers deep,
the oldest being the "*reptilian*,"
the second the "*neo-mammalian*."
The third layer, the "*neo-cortex*,"
is the newest and is a thin crust covering the other two layers
of the brain. I was hopeful I could dig around in my old,
reptilian brain cells where guttural archetypes, as well as
ancient hunting and gathering instincts
were

perhaps

swirling around,
longing,
begging to be consulted.

I had now glimmered one tiny hint, one tiny shard of evidence
and I hoped this hint would allow me to find my way into
these old, mystic, primal thoughts.

I felt unprepared.

" The only remark of nature is
its silence,
but that is not because
the world around us has nothing to say.
It is because we come unequipped
with ears to hear."

Paul Gruchow.

HINT N°2

I started my day intent on visiting the rather grotesque set of sculptures in Lucas, Kansas, known as the Garden of Eden. A place that always made me think of Sherwood Anderson and obsession,

as he writes,

"The subject would become so big in his mind that he himself would be in danger of becoming a grotesque."

I was in danger of becoming a grotesque myself,
I just didn't know this yet.
While heading southeast
from the Black Hills
and the earthy mounds
of the Badlands
I decided to stop
in the unincorporated
village of Round Rock,
Kansas, nestled
up alongside
the slumbering
f l o w
of the South Fork
of the Solomon River.
I was in need of a rest.

Pulling in to the center of the village, I was pleased and a bit surprised to spot a used bookstore. Enjoying the smell of old paper and being a collector of regional-based, natural history essays and odd, local short stories, I was excited at the chance to browse this off-the-beaten-trail location.

Stepping out of my car, I felt the prairie wind that bounced and rattled the metal signs around me. Recalling my friend Dewmore Max's comment with a sly grin—"*Wind only blows around here twice a year, six months from the south, six months from the north.*" I gave a quick shake of my head, stretched my back and travel weary legs until I could feel my lower spine pop. I looked off to the distance at a line of high and heaven-reaching cumulonimbus clouds in the southwestern sky.

Entering the Scratch Pad Bookshop I heard a faint, but friendly, *"Hello"* emerge from what looked to be a middle-aged man, his face deeply buried in an old issue of a numerology magazine, wearing a shirt that said,

"Livin' like a prime number."

I noticed he would occasionally spin in his chair and reach for some oyster crackers to eat, all the while uttering numerical values under his breath. He seemed mostly uninterested in my arrival. There was no music, no television, no radio being played—the store was entirely silent except for the store keeper's mumbling chatter about prime numbers and the value of one. After some browsing I discovered a fascinating publication, which in all my searches for writings on herons, I had never encountered:

Nesting Habits & Ornithological Constellations of the Great Blue Heron in the Mid-Prairie Regions (*Holiseventh Press, Lawrence, Kansas, 1933*),

authored by Dr. Horatio Flatstone, Department of Ornithology and Comparative Literature at what I knew was the now-defunct Nemaha State University, once considered the pinnacle of higher education in the midst of the Flint Hills and the tall grass prairie.

I pulled the publication off the shelf and noticed the entire manuscript had yet to be trimmed along the outer edges. Without any consideration of price, I made my way to the front of the store, quickly paying whatever amount the shopkeeper told me, and exited the front door in a befuddled and anxious state of mind. Standing beside the front door of my car, I felt my breath return. I looked over and noticed a picnic table and my heart slowed down. I moved over to the table, from where I could see and hear the Solomon River, sat down and with my pocket knife cut the book open and began to read.

The small publication was crammed full of revelations, significantly aiding my years of countless premonitions on the evolution and lore of the great blue heron. I suppose I should add I entirely forgot about visiting the concrete Garden of Eden. I spent the remainder of the day reading my newly-found publication with an urgency and sense of curiosity no book had previously provided. The reading was fairly dense, not entirely straightforward and heavily laced with metaphors and unconventional, yet remarkably deft, conclusions. As I read along, I had to slice open each new page which was appropriate as I did feel I was peeling forth secrets. To say I was entirely engrossed in the reading would be misleading. If a tornado had ripped right through during those next few hours I am sure I would not have noticed, just whisked, lifted, and swirled away to a new location. I felt a wild doctrine was being opened up to me, that I was in flight above the earth amongst the towering prairie clouds.

Finishing the book I looked around and saw three great blue herons flying overhead as the sun went down, no doubt returning to a well concealed rookery nearby. I returned to my car and raced down the highway toward my home in
Viriditas, Kansas, near the border line between Leavenworth
and Jefferson counties.
I needed to go to "*my*" rookery and
pay more attention
to a hollow,
old sycamore tree
I had been passing
on my forays to the birds.
There was one particular giant tree
which had always caught my attention, but now,
thanks to Horatio Flatstone,
I understood why.

SHe may have to steer his way home
through the dark
by the north Star, and she will feel
himself to some degrees nearer the star for having lost
his way on the
earth." /

Henry David Thoreau.

Ages Ago

On a silent spring evening during the Miocene, some fourteen million years ago, amidst the bloom of hardy woodland flowers, what appeared to be a constellation of great blue herons began forming in the northern sky. Great blue herons were being hurled out of the dense middle of the earth, one by one, through the hollowed trunk of a giant sycamore tree. Bird after bird heaved in tight and curled-up fashion where they became visible against the backdrop of the Milky Way. This release of birds went on nineteen hours without interruption—each bird slightly different from another, just as every wind that blows is an entirely unique movement. Some great blues had blotches of crimson on their bills, others long white plume feathers. Still others were glossed in powdery layers of fossilized sea salt.

Having been concocted in alchemical fashion through the fusion of earthly elements—way down in darkness where gold is believed to form, congeal, churn, and develop so slowly—the great blue herons were being released from out of the earth to embark upon a journey that would involve living in a sacred realm—just above the ground, very next to clouds, in sight of the sun, while resting on a pillow of invisible air amidst the tips of tree branches and the soft cushion of river bed. One can hardly turn these birds into angels, but there is no doubt they live in the third realm of the spheres, in a spot where they can hear and see the Gods

as they move around within the manifested, physical world.
Their initial mission was,
as Aristotle the ancient Greek might have proclaimed,

to go and live in a state of perfect being.

As with anything deemed perfect there was no more than an instant of paradise in the air once the thin and wispy herons reached the Milky Way. Granted, this all happened so long ago there is no way to know for certain how the night sky looked that evening,* but one has to imagine that the herons glowed in a magnificent pattern, blazing with their long necks tightly compacted, poised and ready to bark out loud and take fly. Their constellation persisted just one night and one night only before the great blues took flight and glided neither further up in the sky, nor back into the depths of the earth, but instead took roost near the surface of the earth, procreating in the tips of the highest trees, taking food from out of the ripples of mud and water, snatching small rodents from time to time.

Creating themselves as beings upon earth, or in the spirit of Nietzsche, living as if,

"the world is a work of art that gives birth to itself."

The herons understood that to remain up in the sky was too "perfect." Living as mere twinkles, millions of light years away from the earth, would provide an uninteresting and continuous blandness.

Paul Shepard writes that

"perfection insinuates a cloying monotony."

---

*Efforts to capture, or even perhaps recapture the arrival of the lights from this constellation, via the speed of light, will no doubt be of great interest to many—those studying the birds, as well as those obscure, yet serious, astronomers who allow themselves to believe in "momentary" constellations.

Considering the habitat of the great blue heron and their lives in isolation, to merely be left on display in the night sky would never have satisfied their reclusive instincts. One has to imagine a couple of things. Being placed in a static position would have been unbearable for a creature that so wants to fly. Secondly, the great blues much prefer to be invisible upon the surface of a single planet in the universe, *resting*, *fetching*, *mating*, *nesting* atop a sycamore tree in a long forgotten, buggy midland valley, than to be on display day and night to whomever and whatever is paying attention in this universe of ours.

Although no device has been created to verify the herons' birth so many centuries ago, there are still ways to explain their origin. Being present as a witness is not such an obstacle as it may appear. Scientific theory has been able to explain, as have stories and rationalizations, many occurrences in the natural world well before the era of human existence. In the book by Dr. Horatio Flatstone, many points are used to explain the origin of the herons. For instance, he utilizes an alchemical evocation from the **Emerald Tablet** to express the herons' origin,

"It ascends from earth to heaven, and again descends into the earth, and receives the powers of the things above and below."

Perhaps this piece of wisdom seems a bit full of mysticism, yet the world does not, even under the most precise and carefully used methods of science, offer any clear understanding of itself. It is rather common knowledge, now, that the world ultimately boils down to having faith in the unknown, not in clinging to what little we think we know.

Albert Camus once stated in clear and profound terms,

38

*"that science that was to teach me everything
ends up in a hypothesis."*

In the whispering, reverent environment of the heron rookery this statement can mean no more, no less than needing faith that these wide-winged species emerged as much from the air as from the soil, as much from fire as from water and in the end needed the bond of an invisible spirit to hatch into reality.

To spot a heron is to spot a balance of the elements.

Horatio is not alone in these thoughts of the great blues coming from out of the center of the earth. Others have said as much in various ways. The need for *"reasonable intuition"* has frequently been used as a manner of understanding and thought.

A small line from author Samuel Butler goes,

"All reason is against it, and all healthy instinct is for it."

Without doubt, I cannot recall how often this comment of Mr. Butler's has crossed my mind during my quest to better know the great blues. I can only imagine that this sort of thinking must have influenced Horatio as well.

Another cryptic naturalist, Edward Abbey said as much,

*"there is a way of being wrong
which is also sometimes necessarily right."*

Dr. Flatstone's publication aptly points out:

"We know that of the great blue heron (Ardea herodias) there consists in structure and attitude equal amounts of both earth and sky."

Perhaps a few additional passages from the doctor's book will better acquaint the reader with this idea:

⊂~ Evidence clearly indicates that a thin and hollow wishbone was broken, precisely and exactly, in half during a tug between the inner sphere of the earth and the outer orb of the sky. The result of which sent these large, grayish blue birds of a prehistoric, reptilian appearance to the surface of the earth where they have existed in the wildest of areas ever since~ not only within isolated habitats, but even to be detached from their own shadows for days and months at a time. The bird, an entirely natural creature, lives alone with its own species as often as possible. Mating season entices the LARGE BIRD uncharacteristically out of its usual behaviors: it barks and kaws and flies in unique and socially induced fashions.

◊

⊂~ These forty-to-fifty-inch-tall birds bear their wildness, perhaps unjustly, with tightly coiled necks. Their column of neck vertebrae is tightly curved in a double folded (S) shape. These bones are interlocked in folds and cusps skillfully held together with unique tendons, allowing the neck to move quickly forward, but just as importantly, providing the neck with such unusually strong power so that it may spring back into a tight position with food in grasp.

◊

⊂~ Their necks appear bound at all times, except when straining to exhibit their strength during mating season. At that time, the males push their necks out painfully straight, as though in victory over gravity, then proceed to fly in large oblong loops, displaying both courage and agility in order to win the approval of an admiring, yet not completely convinced female. The strength (not to mention the sheer necessity of clear, wide open space) needed to perform this demonstration of commitment has proved a useful talent and if interpreted properly, by the female, enables the reproduction of the species to proceed.

◊

⊂~ Each epoch of time is definite in what it produces. The development during the Miocene is that of the grassland with the arrival of the large mountains in the Colorado territory. The development of additional wind then resulted in the spread of grass pollen. This coincided, not surprisingly, with the time frame of the herons' arrival. Similarly, the herons' need for wind to fly, their hollow bones and dependence on the open space of the prairie are all grounds for what amounts to a high correlation of environmental dependence.

◊

Horatio also penned the following passage, prefaced with the comment that it was neither meant to persuade nor dissuade, but may, in relationship to his research, offer a rather "*interesting*" insight toward better understanding his ornithological studies.

:~ I dreamed I was standing up to my knees in a river, and on either side of me were great blue herons. We stood not speaking, but watching the sun rise as though it were a song, a beautiful song of songs emerging slowly from the ground. Although all was silent, I felt I could hear something all the same. The herons, after watching the sun completely peak over the horizon, bobbed their heads a few times, straightened their necks and pointed their bills toward the sky. They lightly danced. I continued to stand still. This was the end of the dream and I wondered about a passage in the Bible, the Song of Solomon, not that this was that song, but perhaps it was a demonstration of love between me and the earth, or representative of the life between species, or better yet, between the land and the herons. Maybe, just maybe, I had glimpsed into the very nature of Love.

In search of more valuable anecdotes on the herons I began to retrace what I could of the work and life of Horatio Flatstone. This was not easy. His documentation was not only far-reaching, but very idiosyncratic, eclectic, and sparse. His little-read book I had chanced upon at the bookstore only included five obscure references, one of which I have not been able to verify.* Another reference, however, was a strangely personal one which I was literally able to locate near the very rookery I was using for my study. Finally, there was one additional *"non-academic"* reference quoting some lines of poetry, of Baudelaire's **Les Fleurs du mal**.

Just as important as Horatio's writings, have been several reproductions of his field drawings. There are also duplications of his handwritten field notes. These notes and drawings appear in the generous and well designed margins of the publication which appears to have been an effort to reproduce both Horatio's naturalist and journalistic attitudes alongside his stoic and ambitious, scholarly research on the great blue heron. The field drawings range from quickly done abstractions of red tailed hawks and sycamore trees, to intricate and colored drawings of heron nests as well as possibilities that may exist deep down in the soil where Horatio and myself have come to believe herons came to life from. Interpreting his drawings, text, short notes, together with information I had already discovered through my own research, I've become convinced of two vital details about the great blues:

1.) I know the very location of the tree from which the first

---

*Clearly identifiable references cited in Horatio Flagstone's publication:
-"Ornithology and the Study of Alephs," Taylor Chukar, *Journal of Ornithology & Rune Stones* (©1912, vol. 32., no.8)
-*Herons: The Great Blue*, Calla Plant & Bailey Bales Productions & CDS Publishers, Inc., Ltd. +/- Esq'rd., ©1903, ff. 89)
-"Works of Celestial Creation in Collaboration with Form Line Art," article in *Cranes Across America*, Patrëkio-Bigg, et. al. (Ascension Press, KS,CH, IN-worldwide-isch, GmbH ©1874, 3rd printing, via lino-pressed oil paper)
-*Birds In Orthodox Russia*, The Hon. & Very Reverend Bishop Carreull von Warrinnik (B. Knorr, Münchner Cycle Haus Q. ©1899.)

1. continued) *great blues entered our world during that long ago night during the Miocene age so many million years ago.*

2.) *I know the spot where the first fossilized remains of the Great Blue are. This spot, I assume, along with Horatio, is worth knowing because the herons flew to it in order to extinguish themselves, following their initial birth from the tree mentioned above. A resting ground to echo their birthing ground.*

Of these two facts the first is more interesting. Yet it is by no means unimportant to know the location of this bird's prehistoric remains. That it turns out to be in the heart of the North American prairie habitat is useful. Habitat is, to a large degree, responsible for a creature's habits (*and vice versa*). This knowledge has provided many stepping stones for me, even though the logic is somewhat spherical in influence. For the record, I should mention that the word "*altar*" was frequently included in the handwritten notes of Horatio. He seemed to believe that the nests, or at least the view of the nests, upward, from his position on earth, offered a vestal shape. Paul Shepard may add to our understanding with a term, "*parochial orbit*," since the birds and their nests seem to suggest a microcosmic-like orbit of their own. The rookery as a whole, and the rounded platform nests themselves are, no doubt, tended by some invisible and natural form of vestal virgin, be it the form of mist, clouds, magical energy, maybe even the beams of ever-reflecting sunlight. After reading Dr. Flatstone's book several times it was clear that the heron was, for Horatio, as much a study of the history and phenomenon of angels, local spirituality   &   magic

as it was the study of ornithology.

With wide outstretched wings, the heron is on a journey amongst the entire spectrum of what are considered the nine realms of heaven. Beneath a crude drawing in Horatio's book was the following passage:

"There is a connection between the angel and the heron which has taken roost in my head. These birds are as much in the air, as of the air. They are, at the least, relatives of wind, dreams, and the invisible."

I also discovered a shared reference between myself and Horatio. There was a local man named Fillmore Grin who was mentioned in Horatio's notes. To my surprise, I had stumbled upon this name on an old, abandoned mailbox near the woodland route I took to the rookery. Right there, by the entrance where I parked, in bold white letters, was **GRiN**. I remembered, at first, admiring the very word Grin, in and of itself, but had no idea that Horatio and I were perhaps researching and examining the very same rookery of blue herons.

Horatio cited Fillmore Grin as, *"an older gentleman who lived right nearby the rookery"* and whom, without the supposed advantages of academia, remained a man with, *"extraordinary understandings and intuitions of natural history and regional lore."* Horatio also stated, *"I never considered Mr. Grin would hold up as a reliable source for my studious activities, but after a period of time I understood that what he knew was more than what was expected of the academic."* One evening I was told about a piece of writing Mr. Grin had created during the last years of his life. I was told that he had only spoke of this *"writing"* with his close friends and family. He had called his writing the **Wild Testament**. Being a rather tight-laced Missouri Synod Lutheran, Fillmore was always a bit nervous about telling anyone his real thoughts on the natural world. He told people in town and in his congregation he was a Lutheran through family tradition, but a naturalist by choice. If he'd been asked to choose between the two, he said he'd rather not have to and that it would be best to leave good enough alone.

I began to question the people in Jefferson township about both Horatio Flatstone and Fillmore Grin. I started by peeking through archives and piles of old newspapers and found nothing. Librarians seemed to know nothing, but the staff was mostly under forty years old so tradition and my curiosity weren't taken all that seriously. I asked around at gas stations and grocery stores, and from time to time someone remembered the name, or that the Grins had lived out of town a ways. Most pieces of information I discovered came during community fundraisers, such as an Optimists' pancake breakfast during the county fair. In fact, it was a Veterans' pork tenderloin dinner that led me to Mr. Flu Bats and sure enough, he had heard of them both. Flu was appropriately named, for his nose seemed to drip all the time and his sneezes were frequent and explosive, his body always seemed to be on the verge of overheating into fever. He was a retired hardware store owner. He didn't honestly think many knew of either Horatio, or Fillmore, but he had served them both at the store and each had revealed they were curious about birds, herons in particular. In Flu's opinion, Horatio had picked up studying the great blue heron's where Fillmore had left off. Both had been drawn to a slow, meandering creek on the Grin farm which ran on into a tight valley for these parts of the country, along the Leavenworth and Jefferson county line. Flu'd been told by Fillmore, when he was buying some knife blades, masking tape, and a pen, about the scrap book/field guide Fillmore had put together. Over time Fillmore confessed to Flu how he had become enamored of some herons he had discovered nearby. In fact, he added, he'd started putting down some ideas on paper "*'bout the world based on his observations of them.*" "*As far as I know,*" added Flu, "*his book of notes was never read by anyone but Horatio, who'd discovered it quite by accident. I imagine the book's still sitting out there in the woods somewhere...*" Flu kind of smirked, "*them Herons sure work the mind over real hard. Someone's always coming along wanting to know just a little bit more about 'em.*"

Flu told me he knew pretty much for certain that Fillmore's writings had been done by hand. He'd never seen the book by Horatio, he went on to say, "*I didn't really expect he was taking it as seriously as he was. He seemed charmed by the birds, but I'd never have guessed he would have written anything.*" Flu elaborated further: "*I expect most of his writing was done while under the influence of some pretty strong arthritis medicine he began having to take the last five years or so of his life, but could be he'd got all obsessed over them and the natural world out there.*" In order to verify and discover the validity of Fillmore and Horatio's hidden book, I began a relentless quest to actually locate the spot where the **Wild Testament** was in hiding.

As luck would have it, I actually found the **Wild Testment**. Horatio had mentioned a hollow and large-trunked sycamore tree in his writing, and this tree had caught my attention time after time during my walks in to the rookery. The tree was right along the trail which I always used to get to the rookery. I had often stopped and admired the significant size of this huge, hollow trunk. Deep in my mind was an inkling that this spot and this tree had to be vital to the area, but never did I imagine its full importance. Yet it was this tree that contained the collection of writings Fillmore called his
Wild Testament.

There was more.

47

This tree was the very stem from which the great blue heron
had been born from during the Miocene so many years before.

It was the center of the heron's world,
and perhaps explains why this rookery keeps drawing
the attention of curious naturalists like myself. I have
since read the *Wild Testament* and just as
importantly, I returned it to its hidden location
There it rests, as you read this now, just as
Mr. Grin placed it and where Horatio found,
read, and returned it. It truly felt like the birds
and trees and wind were keeping a close watch
on me while I read. For the record, I never
removed the document from the forest.
I read it in the woods where
it was written

and only wrote out a few notes to keep in mind the parts
I found absolutely fascinating.

The esoteric volume was sparsely written, a bit erratic, but firmly connected with the local environment. All references were to things visible within a couple hundred yards from where I sat—mention of the small creek, seasonal plant varieties and such. There were no comparisons made with places like California, or Europe. What set the book apart from other books was a strong reliance on common-sense and astute observation. The book proved the importance of this particular place on the earth. The book was anything but boring. There were no rambling digressions. The hand-writing was dark and the lead of the pencil and pen had left imprints in the paper. The forms were labored, not flowing. The **O**'s were more rectangular than circular. Mistakes weren't erased, but either written over or scribbled across to correct. Any prior thoughts I had of Fillmore being in some way deranged, or of being a good-for-nothing eccentric, left my mind. Instead he became a genuinely good-natured, highly aware local hermit, engrossed in a close and intimate observation of the immediate world around him. He seemed in harmony with the *natural*, *spiritual*, *psychic*, *mystic*, and *meteorological*, he even seemed at one with the colors and odors around him. I marveled at the manner in which he had been able to stand back and observe the area which contained the great blue heron rookery. Fillmore had obviously watched and studied the birds intently over decades. He didn't comment on the herons as a group, but had started a rather interesting and peculiar naming of the birds as though they were Angels, Saints, and Prophets. He assigned each creature a name and a piece of holy,
Wild Testament
scripture.

49

Snippets of writing, like seeds poised to germinate, were items he had dreamed of. Fillmore seemed able to probe the very habits of raindrops, which, like the great blues, returned each year—the rain to regenerate new life, the herons to sit atop their thrones at the back of the valley. Each element of the rookery was capable of speaking and even though he was aware the herons and the rain didn't return just for him Fillmore pretended they did and worshipped the land because he knew if he cared for the land, then he was caring for the birds. If Fillmore were able to please the birds then they would tell him things and if he could just do everything right, then they would reveal magic and truth and comfort and grace. For each bird, each nest, each tree contained stories of the land. He felt the world in these birds as a liturgy. The following passages are excerpts from the *Wild Testament* which I found to be fascinating, make of them what you can.

I will include a few short examples below:

† via **Saint Angus Dew** *(the one with the extra long plume feathers)* Heaven must surely be made of memories, where the dearest details loom, then visit and return, recalled as clear as a song of the northern loon

† via **Prophet Huett Longmaul**, aka **Sir Seth**, *(the one with the brightly colored beak)*: Listening doesn't mean waiting for your chance to speak.

† As told by **Saintess Ah-Ha**: The rain here is the rain of there. The sun here is the sun of there. The cry here is the cry of there. The cloud here is the cloud of there. The hopes here are the

hopes of there. I know as anyone knows and know of what anyone will ever know. All of the time, I know I knowest all of this is true.

† As said by **Seraphim Rufus Splatter** (while all six of his extraordinary wings did flutter). The prophet shall be of a different form and odor, neither camouflaged nor ashamed. Barred and in no way slippery. The prophet shall leave footprints which have no replication; with a lingering scent of ash and bacon. Feet tipped with clear, rounded, white nails, but for the right, third digit, it shall be tipped with the color gold.

† **Guardian Angel Azlea** (she landed on her nest with a sense of balance not seen in any other) uttered and I repeat her words precisely, "call this world a Wild Tes/a/Ment, Fillmore." She was influenced somewhat by her retired Southern Baptist mate, Thelbert D. Ogoleby. She believed, and reverently so that, "Religion is more about paying your bills on time than reciting the Lord's Prayer on Sunday. This, mixed with knowing the angle of the sun, makes all the difference in the world."

† **Saintess Sudden**, born of an instant, tricky mechanic of water, fire, earth, and air, and was a vowel messenger. She who seasoned with pinches of holy spirit, would utter no more, no less than "a e i o u," but slowly she would go,

" aaaay yyy Eeee'e'e Fiiiiiii Iiiiii Ohh hhhhh youuuu ..."

† **Saint Emo** sayeth perched from well-polished sycamore branch—the wild comes straight in through the eye, and the eye is fully trained, not just in night vision, but in hypnotics too. Seeing as wind blows, knowing as pollen knows, just when and where each birth awaits arrival.

† **Bishop Blind**, Don't be surprised==sight awaits you in the trunks of the trees, ears in the bends of the grass.

"Creation not only exists,
it also discharges truth."

Gerhard von Rad.

Exploring Pre-Historic

In every love affair there is a threat   of the   fantastic as well as the potential for complete   and   devastating heartbreak. Such is my interest with the   great   blue heron. Placing my deepest concerns with this creature   has been wide and far reaching. Having grasped on to   them   as a way into the heart of the natural world, I've   discovered   that herons have brought ecstatic   visions and epiphanies of a surreal   nature to me. Their simple, yet complex, reptilian appearance has caused me to question my   sanity. Theodore Roszak suggests that   quest ing to be amidst other creatures

is

"where many might say sanity leaves off: at the threshold of the nonhuman world."

I have to admit I am thirsty for this "*insanity*" though, am drooling in a maniacal way for a glimpse of a world filled with herons, especially if that would make me ripe with crazy and enlightened forms of magic and understanding. If only they could allow me to tune into the many scents floating in the air, or become able to hear silence, then, without question I'd be the luckiest man alive. Yet, I am not expectant of a miracle. I am only slightly hopeful the herons may emit a pinch of contagious magic over me which I could inhale, but I know better.

As Paul Gruchow says,

"the only remark of nature is its silence, but that is not because the world around us has nothing to say. It's because we come unequipped with ears to hear."

I accept my limitations and take comfort in wonder, awe, and speculation. I think nothing of seeing the grove of sycamore trees where these birds reside and aching with confusion, spinning in vertigo. I don't believe that a person can inhabit the realm of the rookery and the herons, and the sycamores without reverie.

Roszak adds that seeing the nonhuman world places us

within

"our most private spiritual travail."

Dr. Flatstone, Fillmore Grin, and I are evidence of this, and we are not alone.

Many people quest after different sorts of animal forms as well as plant and even fungi species in order to try and discover our ties to some long-ago, now forgotten language. That enlightenment takes the shape of animals, can come during horrific weather, on the tips of mountains is not strange at all. Our current version of modern human life has created a separation between mind and matter (*not to mention that which matters*), and it seems every day I hope that we are riding the crest of the heavenly spheres and that soon our language and actions and values will return to a sustainable, less consumptive state. Hope that our precambrian minds and genes will awake from their slumber and once again react to the subtle chirp of a bird. Our itching scalps will

remind us that rain is on the way. There seems to me, as I walk
in to see the herons and am able to spot iris, mushrooms, and
creek water moving, that our basic alchemy is disturbed—
our above seems to be torn from our below.
There is no way to underestimate the teachings of the mystics
and their love of inspiration. Their belief that
insightful flashes of knowledge and intuition
could be tied to the
workings of the color green,

{
Fearlessly quest
to find the place between
sunset and the ground
where the ferocious color green
straps the earth with
wrappings of sinuous root
}

the light of sun,
the glow of the moon,
and that fire, water, earth, and air
were accurate and sustainable
for such a long and enduring period of time,
seems to me,
something that should not be discarded so lightly.

Birds have always been considered flashes of deep insight.
Landscape painters, such as Hieronymous Bosch, have *always*
wanted to depict the world as though they were birds. Aus-
picion, need we be reminded, is the bird presenting clues,
answers, responses to our dreams. By walking to the top of hills
and mountains to accentuate the view and by using grand and
ephemeral prospects to present their interpretations, painters
aim to present the world as if angels, birds, or ghosts.

I feel like a child, or perhaps remember being a child,
when in the presence of the great blue herons. Once again

inundated with the thrill of special outdoor places where I used to scurry away to in the cold fall weather as a ten-year-old; on a compost heap, or along a limestone wall out of winter wind, warmed by the seeping, low lowering sun. Other times I would wander in the snow, following a subliminal, or an animal's trail, to an opening in the woods where I would watch the sun descend and the earth would start to glow a dark and deep, metal ore-like color. I lived more in make-believe than in reality, but certainly not less in truth than I do now. My world was entirely true and imagined at the same time. All was candy, greened with sunlight, spiced with the gentle coos of the mourning dove.

Remembering this now,
I find myself recollecting a poem of e.e. cummings:

i thank You God for most this amazing
day: for the leaping greenly spirits of trees
and a blue true dream of sky; and for everything
which is natural which is infinite which is yes.

There is a starting point for all this reverie
and belief around these herons.
Although mentioned earlier, it is worth repeating, that Dr.
Flatstone makes mention of the tremendously wide-trunked
sycamore tree found at the beginning of his journey to the
heron rookery. This hollow and enormous tree,
he states to be,

"the very hole through which the herons emerged to create their brief
constellation so many years ago."

Aware that this sounds as likely as a hurricane in central
Kansas, I will explain what I found.

59

Peering into the darkened cavern of this gigantic sycamore I distinctly observe what appear to be the scrapes of claws and the coloring of feathers rubbed off on the trunk's inner surfaces. Following the angle of the tree's trunk I can postulate the flight into space of the birds, and at night, with my eyes squinting, can envision where their light will emerge in a few million years. I shout down the hollow tunnel. Standing before this tree trunk, knowingly, I am aware my call must travel an incalculable depth before a reply is heard. I knew this tree trunk, this alter of the natural world, and I waited because I had let all of my beliefs go—I had become full of faith.

Zen Master Alan Watts declared:

"Belief clings, but faith lets go."

Just as it may have been for Horatio, this giant tree marks the beginning of my great blue heron journey. This sycamore is what first tickled my mind that something wholly unique existed nearby. The tree seems to prophesy, in hermetic and mystic fashion, an understanding of the region. There are infinities of all sizes, shapes, and forms located around this tree. Thinking about the world is easy—everything around me tells a story of what it is like to live right here: now, then, and tomorrow. I reach back in my memory to recall a single point which contains everything. There is a story by Jorge Luis Borges entitled **The Aleph**, in which the aleph is explained in such a way as to make the dictionary useless.

Borges says of the aleph,

"the sum total of the spatial universe is to be found in a tiny shining sphere barely over an inch across."

Recognition of such a spot

would come to a person instantaneously upon seeing it. I have chosen—for the joy and the agony which will come my way—herons on the tips of sycamore trees, their nests, flight, and actions to be my mentors and spirit guides, my aleph. I know this means all things will stretch in beautiful confusion with no end in sight. I consider how the world is full of an unlimited supply of holiness and this thought makes my momentary life seem inexplicable. On a journey, then, past this hermetic tree, I follow the direction of the creek beside me, gazing upward and forward in anticipation toward my holy land—the rookery. It is purely amazing how well the birds blend their long necks, their arching flight and spectacular nests into their surroundings. It is not long before I spot a few of the birds in flight, *landing, flying, barking, squawking, frahhwking* in spring busyness. My heart churns like a geyser.

I take a deep breath and prepare to enter sacred ground.

As I get nearer and nearer, I finally feel no more than the
whiff of a whisper, the lightest puff
of the letter   "   "

in my emptied mind.

I bow, sit down, watch, listen,
and contemplate with all my senses wrapped together.
Peeking up to view the birds I always feel slightly invasive,
as though spying on someone who would be offended at
my peering.

This time I notice one of the great blues, perched on the inner cup of a nest, sitting still amongst the flights and flurry of other herons, peering directly at me

the bird does not move

or twitch

or seem self conscious

it only keeps staring into my eyes

we look at each other, and it seems as though

we communicate with our hearts

not our minds,

or our ears,

or our mouths.

I wonder if we are both curious why the other is entering what seems to be a deep and lucid state of meditation. After a span of maybe twenty minutes, this single great blue utters a high pitched whistle. An approval? I am not certain. I grin, in approval. However, what does become clear is that there is a reversal of my intention on this journey, which has taken me by surprise. I feel as though immersed in warm soft water, for I have become the observed. I have heard that to observe nature is as though being part of scripture, so what does it mean to become the observed?

I reason this is why Dr. Flatstone included the small portion from the poet Baudelaire:

"We walk through the forests of physical things that are also spiritual things that look on us with affectionate looks."

"Curiosity cannot receive a
genuine response
to what it investigates
if the person cannot
tolerate emotional disturbance."

Shierry Weber Nicholsen.

$\mathcal{T}he\, \mathcal{F}$LAVOR $_{of}$ $\mathcal{B}$RASS

Discovery of the great blue herons' nests is not possible without careful attention. These creatures of the air inhabit silent spots at the back of wilderness, where creeks slide each moment through stands of phosphoric and glowing, flaking, and chipping sycamore trees.

The heron is a wild creature and a majestic recluse who refuses to reside where other creatures, especially humans, or another of its major antagonists, the bald eagle, will find it. The herons' nests are intended to be secrets. Looking for them is a guessing game.

I have been lucky to observe herons near enough to hear them breathing. Their gaze is something akin to pure emotion—not so much sadness, glee, or impatience, but a smooth and curling weave of morning fog, twisting skyward, joining thin veiled cumulus clouds toward infinity. The heron's yellow-edged eyes raise the hairs on my arms and neck and prick goose bumps on my skin. The stare of this bird is not so much at me, as into me. I imagine it thinks my lungs would taste exceptional, as easy to scoop from me as a tadpole out of the Kaw River. What I have observed may not be great or earth-shattering, and perhaps the herons' lives are considered trivial by others, however, I feel comfort in the words of Lao Tsu,

"See simplicity in the complicated.
Achieve greatness in little things."

When the heron moves its gaze off me and lifts one foot gently out of the water, forward, without rippling the shallow water it is standing in, it makes as much noise as grass seed growing, as the commotion of an ant sneezing. I continue to stare, and no thoughts enter my mind. I am fixated on the heron's every move and feather. A duck flies in from overhead and breaks my trance. At the same instant, the heron flails and flaps away.

My imagination runs rampant—are these birds long-ago dwarfs with wings?
I reach this odd conclusion:
the heron seems to be living in a different time and place from me.
I wonder:
is the blue heron in search of solitude, or is the blue heron trying to find its way out of solitude?
They resemble ancient and austere hermits on a secret, mystical journey while dwelling at the center of the world.

The great blue heron possesses a pair of wings big enough to shadow an entire valley. When spooked off the branches of a high rising sycamore tree they let loose guttural belches—

grumbly, bedrock laden

sounding more like roots than the mere movement of feathers
and air.

Long tendril-legs place this bird as much as four-and-a-half-feet off the ground. These slender legs allow the bird to miss the ruffle of wind, while providing a method to move without ripple through high water. Often considered a coarse creature with leathery legs and feet, the heron also displays a committed sense of honor and delicacy. For instance, the male heron finalizes its marriage each spring by offering the female a twig to add to the nest.

In moments of prenuptial bliss, the heron will fly three or four minutes, in a giant circle, four to five hundred yards wide, neck outstretched, circling in the hemisphere as though creating a wedding band in the sky. An adept creature of the Middle West, a heron needs vast and isolated air space in which to live, only feeling at home in areas such as Northeast Kansas, with its wide-open landscape and little-known tree-filled valleys. The great blue is a primeval species. It reminds people of some sort of reptile. The shape of its head and neck, together with lightly crimson legs, make it appear somewhat like the tongue of a lizard.

Perched in a silent, isolated world amongst the bloom of woodland flowers, the birds hide nothing. They boldly display primal instincts—*tapping, snapping, touching,* and *bowing* their bills with one another. The male clasps the neck of the female with his long orangish bill while mating. This is definitely not a position to take lightly. The bill of the heron is a dangerously sharp weapon, serrated along the edges, and can be catapulted forward with the energy contained in its eighteen-to-twenty-inch neck—a neck fully spring-loaded with a network of ferocious muscles. It would be no problem at all for a heron to puncture right through the skull of a man or woman.

The bird is easily insulted by intrusion. When I spot a heron along a river while canoeing or on my way into the rookery, I notice there is no hesitation in the way the bird churns out a large gobbet of runny white guano as its long legs trail and wide wings fiercely flap and flap. In a light wind, I often pick up the slightest whiff of the heron's breath, revealing an odor I can best describe as that of thick, green moss on the shady side of tree bark, an unctuous aroma additionally spiced with the pungency of worm casings and piles of dew-soaked cedar shavings and a pinch of chanterelle mushroom.

Beneath a heron's nest fall the bones of the unsuccessful.
In survival of the fittest fashion, the newborns begin
battle early in life for pieces of regurgitated food offered by their
parents. In these fights of subsistence, siblings often push
brother or sister from the highest tips of the tall trees, thus
creating compost for the sycamore trees towering above. This
is a rude lesson in sympathetic magic—the herons sacrificing
themselves for their local environment,
thanking the trees and creek
for their role in their survival.
To live as a sycamore tree,
or a heron
is inherently lonely.

My admiration for the great blue is as intense
as its evolution has been.
I believe that if I were offered
a cup of heron blood to drink,
I would do so without hesitation.

I am most alive when I am in their presence.
The intimacy I feel with these birds suggests
I am involved
in a form of initiation.

I am transported through the boundaries
between cultured humanity and natural wildness.
Instead of needing money and worrying
about how my neighbor mows his lawn,
I am engrossed in the basest ingredients of the greedy,
full-blooded harmony
of the entire world.

My body and mind go plunging into the workings
of the clouds and wind,

to observe the tips of the heron's wings,
whose ends bend and fall with the air when flying.

Each time I visit the rookery,
I feel these things inside me.
I close my eyes and see fire and
water, earth and air.
I sense a holy spirit.

I believe there is a value in the invisible,
whether for the invisibility itself,
or for some lesson coming which I can't see.
I become enveloped in awe and get carried away.
Going to where time moves much too slowly to even exist.
I am transposed to where deep, long ago stories of the land
reside.
To that wild place where poet
W. S. Merwin suggests
resides the realm of our

"forgotten language."

Standing beneath a heron's nest,
stooping over and picking up one of the infant's bones,
my armpits begin to drip, and my lips become dry.
I rummage through my mind, raise my eyebrows,
and hear a line
of
William Faulkner echo around inside my ears:

"A flavor like brass in the sudden run of his Saliva, a hard sharp

constriction either in his brain or his stomach,

he could not tell which and it didn't matter."

71

As though these words were prayer,
I go over them
again

&

again.

My hands and fingers constrict with the thought.

This place is love
and instinct
made of first-born thoughts.

Even as I experience this place,
I begin to long for it to
continue.

I swallow, my mouth seems taut,
a metallic flavor feels to be upon my tongue.

This prehistoric world of the great blue
provides another vision—a great blue walks up beside me, and
we meditate on the flow of water. The earth   stalls, and I spot
frogs moving between beams of sunlight in the water. I see in
the reflections of the creek water   that the great blue beside me
is cloaked in a robe of   gray and blue, preened and covered
with waterproof   dust, gleaming with a robust and fluttering
sheen in the evening sunshine as though a star.   This heron is a
prophet of the prehistoric—dressed with wings and feathers.
Moving out of my trance, I   hear feathered wings flap hard,
and although I look   quickly for the bird,

even try to spot a

moving

shadow,

I see

nothing.

Ecologist

and

philosopher

David

Abram

professed,

"To listen

to the forest

is also,

primordially,

to feel oneself listened to by the forest."

And so I stand, looking and wondering if the great blue can
hear what I hear. Can the heron hear my heart beating loudly?

"Magic, then, in its primordial sense,
is the experience of existing
in a world made up
of
multiple intelligences."

David Abram.

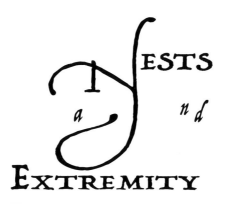 NESTS and EXTREMITY

On average, the clutch of eggs laid by the great blue heron is four. While one of the bigger bird species, the size of the great blue's egg is smaller than might be expected. Given that this species of heron stands much taller than the screech owl, a ten-inch bird, it seems strange that the screech owl's egg is actually larger. In the alchemical world, this detail is not insignificant. The great blue heron's egg must necessarily obtain a highly concentrated life force, maybe inside the eggshell rests a potion comprised of helium, which manifests upon birth, so that when the small baby heron makes contact with, first breathes, the air surrounding the rookery, an expansion occurs unlike that of the screech owl.

It is likely the great blue goes through two stages of imprinting. The baby heron's first imprint is with their parents. The second imprint starts soon thereafter, as soon as their eyes can clearly discern depth-of-field. This imprint is with the long angular branches of the sycamore tree, the smell of creek water filtered across limestone, and the sounds of earthworms digging in the rich soil beneath the herons' nests. If you try to distinguish the shape of the grown heron's neck and legs from the branches of a sycamore tree, it becomes clear that the two are remarkably similar.

The great blue's eggshell is a careful blending of pale blue with the lightest faintest tint of green. This coloring allows the egg to merge with their surroundings: the large bird's piecemealed, scattered, palimpsested platform nests among the trunks of the sycamore trees. This evolutionary coloring of the egg is an act of pure genius. I imagine that the slightest coloring of the eggs may cause a crow to pause just long enough, confused as to whether the eggs are leaves, a twig, or a chunk of sycamore bark, and thus keep an unborn heron from becoming just a bite to eat. In reality, I'm told, it rarely works this way. The crows and eagles aren't very confused.

ii.

Sir

James George Frazer, author of *The*

Golden Bough, explained that "*primitive man takes his soul out of his body and deposits it for security in some snug spot, intending to replace it in his body when the danger is past or...he may be content to leave his soul there permanently*." There is something startling and intriguing about this idea of a soul external, of the ability to place a soul outside the self somewhere in the wider world. This act sounds at the very same instant both remarkably possible and yet dauntingly impossible.

Could any of us be so lucky as to place our souls off to the side and let them rest unattended? Could we be so lucky as to set aside our soul and let it soak in the moon's gentle creamy reflections, or allow our soul to be enriched inside a fox den, or secured and swirling in an eddy of cool spring creek water? Such thoughts seem absolutely too luxurious, but certainly worth wishing for.

When I think of the amount of misdirected momentum that our "modern" life has created, I know that something as intricate, delicate, and precise as placing a soul externally would involve far too much patience to be accomplished by a human being. Nine-and-a-half out of ten of us are too concerned about paying mortgages or wondering about the next special at the super-duper-mart-o-rama to contemplate a soul at all.

A soul is unique and needs to be in balance—not embraced for just one sudden moment—with sustaining thought and enduring care, using a process of ritual. This is not how we are inclined to live. There is a lack of self-sufficiency and, as a result, a loss of personal empowerment.

Robert Wolf,
sums our predicament up well:

"[People] are no longer able to see things as aspects of Infinity, but see all things as finite and measurable."

Placing the soul requires that we make the commitment of our life, which is perhaps as infinite a commitment as we can make. The soul of the heron is outdoors and hiding and living comfortably with infinity. Their options are wind and rain, sun and stone, dirt or leaves. Their world is not one of red lights, due dates, warranties, or dial tones. What comes their way is not nearly as important as being able to survive what comes their way. Perhaps their days are slower than ours, not broken down in seconds and minutes but in sunlight to sunset. Summer to fall. Full sun to shadow.

Their migrations are based on the angle of the sun, but nothing in the heron's life is in anyway less complex than ours. Somewhere in my ancient, latent mind I know placing the soul externally is all-important. I crave the compassion and insight required to integrate a soul to the burl of an oak tree, wish to understand the spiritual and invisible acts required. I know the idea rests in me somewhere since the very notion of placing a soul is a conundrum, like a riddle with the answer on the tip of my tongue. It sounds so right, yet at the same moment *impossible*.

Taoist Lao Tsu states,

"The easy way seems hard"

Placing the soul externally is not difficult.
Just figure out how and where.

If any living thing could place a soul externally, it would be the great blue, this sleek and persistent prophet of the prehistoric. Yet the great blue is not a normal prophet. They are prophets of the extreme, and in their presence we are awe-struck, momentarily we go speechless. Historian of thought Allan Megill points out that,

"The prophets of extremity put up a distorting mirror against our world."

I have come to believe that the great blues, without trying

(*to continue quoting Megill*),

"help us break out from a deadening routine, from the petrification."

When the herons fly away, after a quick glimpse of their movement, we agonize and question their natural existence as if we know that somewhere in our deep pulse we once knew the songs of richly sedimented sand-bars, once knew how to walk like a heron just as well as we now read an issue of the daily newspaper.

American philosopher William Hocking wrote,

"The mystic in historic action is termed the prophet."

I truly believe this to be the case of the great blue.

In the words of William Everson,

"The mystic speaks.
...Obsessed by enchantment, tantalized by the
imperceptible, he yields his reason to his instinct."

Longevity is needed in order to place, revisit, and refresh the soul external, which is exactly the point. For eons, humans were in close communication with the natural variety and sensual aspects of life on earth, not just with themselves and their self-created systems and techniques. The great blues, by nesting in the same spots year after year, are involving themselves in ritual, which evokes a power of place and proves importance.

Placing a soul externally requires an uncommon ability to be cloaked in secrecy. A blue heron's rookery is an ideal spot, since they nest and mate and raise their young only when they have reason to believe they will be amidst complete privacy. Not only this, but it can't be just a passing detail that the herons have picked the sycamore tree, for one thing, it is a long lived tree which records its history in its appearance: limbs & trunks that are tattered, bent, & gnarled with chips of bark that fall and peel & pile upon the ground. Beyond this, the oldest remains, as mentioned by Horatio Flatstone, of the great blues rest on the vast open space of the Great Plains in Nebraska, a day's flight from their birth place on the earth.

At first it is not necessary to associate the great blue heron with the sycamore tree; it just happens that both I and Dr. Flatstone have. The interesting correlation between the two can be examined by theories of a soul external. As mentioned, the soul external is a magical placement, properly understood best in the context of perception and longevity. The sycamore tree can play host to both of these needs since it is the longest living deciduous tree species in the Midwestern region, living well beyond the spans of memory. During this time, a siege of herons can certainly invoke the time needed to attend to any special needs that the soul external may require. Transferring, for example, the soul from one spot to another, from one limb to the next as it evolves. The tree, like the heron, is able to stand as native to one particular spot. Is able to feed off of what a particular spot has to offer. Satisfied with the rain that comes during the year; satisfied with what sunshine comes its way, neither hoping for more, nor wishing for less. Living from what actually happens. Letting these years seep and create and develop allows for a soul as unique as the flavor of wild cherries from one place in a woodland to the next. The sycamore drops its leaves, its seeds, and particular acids and medicines into the soil: all of which weave and form a unique place. As for the oldest remains of the great blue heron, that they are to be found in the earth of the Great Plains could be considered a coincidence, but it is doubtful. This makes perfect sense for a host of good reasons. The Midwest is hardly even thought of as any place by most people of the world, yet it is a coveted fly zone for birds, storms, and butterflies.

The precise location of the early remains are located at the Observation Quarry and indicate this early genus type is at least fourteen million years old. Think how many migratory flights have gone on beneath the watch and wings of the great blue, then consider how many times a sycamore tree has been used as a nest. The vast open plains are sometimes referred to as the forgotten coast or, in older maps of the United States, as the Great American Desert. My suspicion is that the heron loves this sort of thinking. If the herons were able to discern statistics and find out that population totals were declining in Kansas or Nebraska, they would probably add an extra congratulatory belch to their array of noises. Of course, where better to create a constellation for yourself? Blowing out of the ground amidst nothing but the solace of sky above. In a land that is known for being forgotten, lost, and cast away.

Another advantage to residing on the Great Plains is the mating flight of the great blue, an act performed with its neck stretched out, which is not an easy maneuver for the bird. The Plains, however, provide ample space for this wide and peculiar action. Just as the human body is at least half water, so the Great Plains is predominantly sky and open space. A vast, three-to-four-hundred-yard circular flight to impress a female even sounds Midwestern. It's not exactly great pick-up line, or a verbal masterpiece, but it is a strong action that speaks for itself and impresses.

If you do come upon a rookery in a stand of sycamore trees somewhere in Kansas, Iowa, or Nebraska, stop all forward motion, stand still, do not move your shoulder, just twist your head, and eyes to look around. *Spy for small altars hidden in the top branches.*

I agree with Dr. Flatstone on this:

"that a rookery seems tended by a chorus of vestal virgins."

There is a purity, an innocence, and a beauty that expel air, that will mystify speech and thought. This I account for because of the presence of the soul external. Enter reverie, which is an emotion we feel when words go away.

iii.

Having visited the remains of abandoned heron rookeries, I can attest that these spots seem haunted and void of any external souls. Evacuated rookeries are clearly cheated of a sensible inheritance of continuous life. They lack a partnership with mystery and tradition. They are echoes and memories without beat, void of flapping, ominous realms of the sort that once harbored a sensuous and slowly evolving soul external. The partnership between spirit and soul has been removed, and the cause most normally comes from
invasions of human noise,
or worse yet,
is a result of the soul external's
discovery.

The magic of the hidden soul, once discovered, goes away. This is a point made quite clear by Sir George Frazer in his **Golden Bough**. Pointing out a couple old stories, from regions such as Cambodia and Russia, will help sum up the state of the rookery once the soul external is discovered by the wrong creature.

A daughter may ask,

"Papa, where is your soul?"

To this simple question Fraser has discovered:

"Sixteen miles from this place, he said, is a tree. Round the tree are tigers, and bears, and scorpions, and snakes; on the top of [the] tree is a very great fat snake; on his head is a little cage;

83

in the cage is a bird; and my soul is in that bird."

When this bird is found and destroyed, so too is the father.
One frequently finds the soul external hidden in trees.
Another example:

*"My death, said he, is far from here
and hard to find, on the wide ocean. In that sea is
an island, and on the island there grows a green oak, and
beneath the oak is an iron chest, and in the chest is a small
basket and in the basket is a hare, and in the hare is a duck,
and in the duck is an egg; and he who finds the egg and breaks it,
kills me at the same time."*

Unfortunately, someone does find the egg and does kill
this man's soul   and thus,   causes his death.

What is fascinating is the tie between the placement of the
soul in trees with life. Through mystic intuition,
I know this heron rookery in Kansas
harbors a soul external.
The place is a sanctuary for deep,
long-lasting and harmonious life.
It is my opinion that it is
the very soul
of the species
Ardea herodias,
the great blue heron.
This place offers clues as to the heron's soul:
there are the crowns and limber shapes of the sycamore tree,
the winding, calming trickle of creek water, filtered through
the top soil and humus of the sycamore's leaves, the remains

and offerings of the herons themselves. There is the blessing of the soft and continual breeze jostling tree tops and the gift of cottonwood's cotton. In this position beneath these nests, amongst the bones strewn on the ground, or inside the trunk of a tree, there is the hum and churning of a private, vital soul external in possession of the scent of the earthly elements, an odor distinctive yet indescribable. I will not, dare not, look for the soul external though. For deep in some spot is a bright, smooth, living item, as if a slowly blinking eye, at rest but growing. A soul spinning in place, on a journey, but not seeming to move.

I believe I have been offered this secret,

in order to give thanks and that I need to protect and avoid being too specific about where this spot is. Somehow, I must share the soul external, but at the same time I must not give the soul away, since this will cause death. There is a level of trust that goes with knowing the soul's location. That the external soul can be placed in animals, inanimate objects, as well as trees, is at the same time helpful and that much more confusing. Does the heron fly with the soul, if so when? Is it able to tend to the soul from other places in a sympathetic way? Or does the great blue need to literally come to these particular spots for a period of time, checking on the soul's condition in the deep roots of the sycamore trees?

This whole soul external issue is complex and endlessly fascinating. Fraser also explains the power of sympathetic magic. This magic is such that the one whom the soul belongs to never needs to retrieve it. Thus, in theory, one could hide a tangible soul in a sacred spot and then travel within the world's most hideous spots, but at no point would the person lose touch with beauty unless someone were to discover and ruin their hidden soul. Through mystery and silence, the soul rests in its secret, sacred spot, safely tended to and cared for.

The comparison to the vestal virgins, tending reverently a fire for eternity becomes appropriate in this regard, as this sort of protection surely allows one to feel the eternity of the soul's safety.

The depth of the great blue's soul external is a miracle. They know of the oceans which once covered this realm of Great Plains. They are not ignorant that this vast landscape once housed peaks of a high reaching mountain range known as the Nemahas. The soul external of the great blue can recall without hesitation the wild stampede of the bison. Not a single oceanic high tide, thunder bolt, or drip of glacier ice has been lost to *Ardea herodias*. Their soul absorbs, churns and contains this landscape and all that has been.
Understanding this will seem too fantastic and
if it were not that I know the great blue to be a prophet,
then I would doubt the pure depth of this.
I mean, after all, what is a prophet,
but
"one who speaks what is unsayable to others,
but once spoken,
immediately carries its own authority?"

In spite of what I can observe and understand of the great blue during its fishing habits, styles of flight, nest creation, mating dances, beak tapping, and migration patterns, it still remains an unknowable creature to me. However, I know that I must listen, watch, and learn all the same, for there is never a time when the great blue is not living out the ways and methods of the wild and prehistoric.

In sync with my thoughts of prophets and herons, I raise my eyesight to the highest tips of the stand of sycamore trees along the trail from the hermetic tree. I recognize the sounds of the downy woodpeckers in the background. I hear a red tail hawk squeal up high in the distance. I notice the light footwork of chickadees and peeps of the nuthatch. Concentrating on hearing the wind overhead, I imagine the depth and placement of the soul external being roosted and tended in this place, where the siege of great blues descend each year, here, on the Great Plains of eastern Kansas, in this remote corner of Jefferson County, along a creek that shall remain unnamed.

I look up to see forty, maybe fifty, even sixty nests globbed together like beaver dams, defying gravity, stick by stick perched and balanced into broad platforms which from below appear rounded as though planets. These nests are built upon year after year, until the wind blows them down, or they simply become so heavy the limb bursts off. How a family of large lanky birds can reside so high in the limbs of a tree makes me delirious with wonder.

The herons' nests, as though full moons above me, are glowing and humming while mixing together the earthly elements of this place: bits of bark, twigs, mud, items from the air and water. Whether dawn or dusk there is no greater thrill than to see these nests when the herons, in search of sunlight-enriched food, appear as though shooting stars, or angels.

I am, again, reminded of the vestal virgins tending the Vestal fire, those pure-hearted souls, attendant for the sake of sacred eternity. I actually believe that there can not be much difference between a soul external and a soul eternal. I know that the external soul is placed in order for rest, protection, and the inheritance of knowledge. I have come to realize that what I call the wild, a heron knows as everyday "*normal.*" We often feel out of place in the world, certainly we are locked out of the natural world by being limited to no more than perception in all we do.

Tara Brach says,

"Feeling separate is an existential trance in which we have forgotten the wholeness of our being."

iv.

The nests radiate an energy. My heart drops, pulling my breath down to my knees. I am undergoing a change. Is wandering amidst the nests of the herons a sacred journey? It is as mysterious a thing as if I were to wake floating with cumulus clouds one morning. I wonder if I should begin praying each morning in their direction. I start to carry relics, make relics, feel a relic myself.

It doesn't really matter how long the soul external has been harbored in this grove of trees, or even how the separation of body, memory, and the soul occurs. The variety of possibilities is so dense and timeless, my brain might as well be wandering an ancient labyrinth. I consider these souls to be holy objects, amulets from times even prior to the Miocene.

I lightly whisper to myself,

"Ashes to ashes... dust to dust."

I am not sure why, except that I feel something here that once was nothing, born from out of mystic sensitivity. Of importance to me is to offer prayer to the heron's soul, to touch the sycamore's trunk, and drink the water moving elements.

Using intuition, simply sitting in one place and looking up, I reflect on my life. It occurs to me that I have laid my eyes on a soul external before. Out of the corner of my eye, lying on a heap of leaves in my wooded childhood valley in Iowa, a chilled early, October morning, hours before my friends would get up, I heard three doves cooing nearby. Lazily, I gazed into this nowhere, but what I discovered instead of doves was a cluster of bright butterflies floating around my head, and instead of waving them away, I felt calm and watched their fluttering shapes wisp and rise and scatter as I tried to focus. The butterflies were not as real as the colors on their wings: incredible blurs of brightly tinted mushy liquid—*blue-gold, green-silver, red-copper, yellow-brass,*

stars flashing tin.

I felt amazed back then,

noth**ing short of fascination and bewilderm**ent.

This became a secret held so tightly

I'd forgotten it **entirely, but now I wanted this** moment back.

Thomas Moore wrote:

"A *spiritual sensibility* rises *directly* out of *the human encounter with the natural world.*"

I had been offered a glimpse into a soul external
when younger by the natural world.

Recovering childhood glory is the journey of the hero. I certainly feel heroic once again as I stand admiring the great blues, just as I did so many years ago when watching what may have, may not have been, the water-colored clump of butterflies. Remembering my childhood encounter with the soul external, it occurs to me that I am living a straight, yet forever curving path up toward the wide hearted open sky above me. Always, ever so slightly, ever so constantly, I am in one way or another preparing for flight, forming the wings of a seraph, becoming a beautifully colored butterfly crossing a threshold in to enlightenment.

I am clinging as narrowly as a cliff swallow's nest to the edges of certainty though. I explore the meanings and location of this thing called the soul external with as much doubt as certainty. If such a thing is as true as I believe, then it is an ancient practice which has been going on thousands and thousands of years, so it should seem obvious, but it's not.

Perhaps because I need to have certainty, belief, grace in my life.

I know this has its possible drawbacks.

What any of us anywhere know is only as certain as a story,

a wish,

or magic.

Even theology,

writes William Gass,

"*appears to be one half fiction* / *one half literary* **criticism**."

I suppose, then, I am one half understanding this great rookery and the soul external to be real, but I am one half wondering if I am not making things up, wishing for what I want in spite of contrary, even non-existent evidence. However, I do not understand this to be a problem, for I agree, conveniently or not, with Señor Jorge Luis Borges, who professed from the library of his mind that,

"*My story will be true to reality, or in any case, my personal memory of reality, which amounts to the same thing.*"

As I gather this sense of certainty and joy, I seem to become almost as quickly full of sorrow. I'm not satisfied with theory, with philosophy, and I feel cheated, because I want to have more intimacy with the beauty of the sycamore trees and the slabs of rock lining the creek. I would like to be closer to the loose sticks lying on the ground, those lucky strands of wood which become parts of the heron's nests.

I take comfort that once humankind did battle to know the world like a snake or the tangles of wild rose vines. Partly inspired by beauty and partly inspired by premonition, I have wished to be swayed in the realm of this rookery by the mystic Hildegard of Bingen, who devised that a place such as this could exist in a soulful way, known through instinct and intuition, generating power from the color and life of that which is green.

The heron is a mystic
in the manner which Hildegard suggests,
since the space where it resides is able to
illuminate the darkness.

That is to say,
each time I visit this spot
I am brought out of myself
and into a new,
"universe with a different quality,
an entirely different world, transcendent and holy."

It may seem overly sentimental to suggest that I have seen the light, or found a holy spirit, yet each exploration into the perches of the great blue does bring me closer to the creativity of the world and how I and all species fit together. Each visit brings me closer and closer to understanding the difference between solitude and silence. I realize watching these large ancient creatures in the woods is, although loud, somehow absolutely silent at the same time. They are similar to wind overhead in the leaves of cottonwoods, are the noise which waves bring after they are created from the silence of the sea.

I have become mesmerized into solitude.

Contemporary writer Kathleen Norris states that
mystic sensibility is able to,

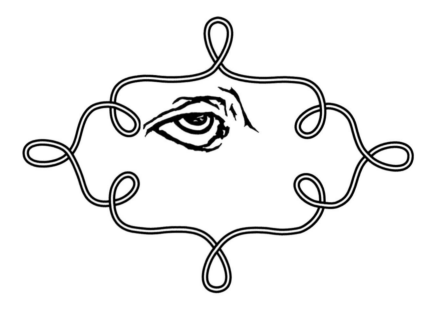

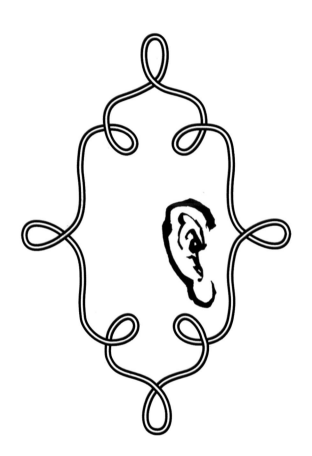

"see, hear and know

simultaneously."

Precisely.

In the *"viriditas"* way of being, there may exist the work of an indefinable God: a deep and unfathomable force of consistency based upon continual creative renewal that I believe comes to roost through mystic sensibility. This is what may be contained in the soul external, who knows? I am satisfied with the bold and brilliant colors of my childhood and the slow glow of faith being born in me with each visit to the rookery. I wish for the greening power to tend me, care for me, keep me growing, full of hope, and sprouting.

This rookery is a wild journey, and fortunately I do not feel the need to travel far. In this sense of place rests the very speck of all things. I am reminded of a story about an old Italian woman from the Fourth Century. This lady revealed a lesson during a visit from St. Sarapion of Sinodite. It turned out that the woman had not moved, not even spoken or nary blinked her eyes, for decades, and as a result had become widely celebrated as a great recluse within the city of Rome.
St. Sarapion, a well-respected wanderer,
went to this lady and wondered,
whispering in her ear,
"Why are you sitting here?"
To which I imagine the old lady
slowly, quietly, replied,
"Sir, do you not see?
I am not sitting here, I am on a journey."
St. Sarapion must surely have felt confused.

How could this lady, just sitting in place, be on a journey. Was she not harboring a soul external? If this thought did occur to St. Sarapion, it must have occurred to him like a revelation that if this lady was in fact on a journey, then he must be busy scrambling in missed directions.

What she was doing was developing a native Tao. The location of the great blues in Viriditas, Kansas, is just this, a teacher of instinct and grace. I remind myself that these nests, these trees, the soul external—none of them are just sitting here, but on a solitary, well-tended, motionless, yet exciting journey.

It is clear, now is the time to investigate the realm of the prophet of the prehistoric. To investigate I suggest staying where you are. Dawns will come to you without any effort whatsoever.
Gather twigs and build a nest in which to place your soul.
Find solitude and then go in to the wild
with your heart content.
Try to find forgotten languages
with incantations able to let loose
magic off our fingertips or through our eye balls.
Remember when the earth was ash and dust when the wind blew and the earth churned and developed without our human thoughts, when art and creation were identical and at once
s   u   r   v   i   v   a   l   .
Keep in mind that the strange is not incorrect,
weird is not
unusual,
funky is not negative and that
*"the imaginal is intermediate
between material and the spiritual."*

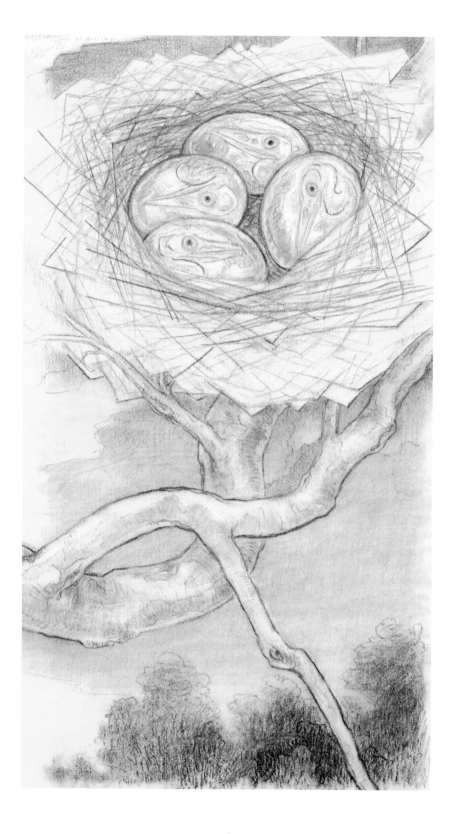

"I am certain of nothing but the holiness

of the heart's affections."

John Keats.

HERMITS, *Silence* & MƛDNESS

Perhaps because he passed away so young, but with such talent, the poet Keats is able to capture the surprises and wonders of the world.

I quote him in relationship to the rookery:

"Negative Capability is when a man is capable of being in uncertainties, mysteries, doubts, without any irritable reaching after facts and reason."

What better way to describe the presence of the rookery and its environment. I accept this spot not as a well-groomed location comfortably laid out for myself, or even the heron, not as a pasture grazed by cattle, not as a perfect garden thoughtfully organized to be as mankind wishes, but as a spot that without courage I would wander to and cut and tangle and draw blood from myself in confusion. The realm of the heron's birthing ground is as wild as wild can be.

Wilderness persists as it is, with no regard for expectations.

Gary Snyder says,

"To speak of wilderness is to speak of wholeness."

In the natural world there are no lies being told.

I come here with a faith of the natural world in my head, not one that congratulates myself as though I were alive and well atop the heap of some evolutionary pyramid, but as someone that rejoices in this sacred spot precisely because I know I become in-line with birds, moles, water,
even
microscopic protozoa.

There is a madness to this wildness. A madness of
originality, but also a madness like that of a hermit.
I am like a *"mad"* man who creates, not like the mad man
who kicks and pounds the world with anger. I revel in the
sympathetic and contagious magic in this place. The beauty
of magic is such that it is not so unreal as we think. In many
ways it is in opposition to spirituality in much the way many
mistakenly believe science and spirit to be. One way of
considering magic is that it is a process of cause and effect,
not at all dependent on blindness, and hope, but predicated
upon actions. I would be a fool to declare that I think magic
is the sole explanation for the earthy world and the charm
of the heron. I would be foolish to declare that blind
faith brings me all I need in relationship to the structure,
beauty, and mystic links the thrones of the herons offer me.
I would be foolish to think that a science will explain
to me the chirps, the squawks, or the clamor as well.

Magic sways the rookery in subtle, but forceful
ways. I pick up a feather of a heron and feel part of the
heron enter me. I sense the well-concealed placement of
the soul external nearby—controlled and nurturing.
These feelings are esoterically alchemical.

If we are to take the mystic, alchemical imagery further we
must suppose the equality of the below and the above. We must
be willing to delve deep and high. William Occam proposed
the
ever-famous Occam's Razor theory
which goes along these lines:

what we know is built upon emptiness,

upon concepts and therefore one can stride straight to the source

through intuitive cognition (Notitia Intuitiva).

How is this of any value?

If we use our intuition we can travel straight to the heron's side and my intuition allows me to find them to be no less than a variety of archangel of the highest rank.

What to make of this reverent bird in this light? The heron becomes a magical form, an angel with two large wings. It is a guardian of the natural world and a friend of Saint Francis. I present these hopeful and beautiful images of the heron just as previous humans have presented all beautiful angels.

As Malcolm Godwin declares at the
conclusion of his book on angels:

"If you really want to see an angel don't look for one outside: they reside within, and so long as human beings seek their own totality and wholeness, the angelic species cannot be endangered."

This is definitely a useful way to see the herons, and perhaps the best way to make use of the spirit which I believe to be all around them.

If I am to tell other people, as Horatio Flatstone and Fillmore Grin did, of the miracles of this rookery, I am already prepared to be shunned and met with peals of laughter and disbelief. Like I said, revealing mad ideas, thoughts, and hopes which can't be fully quantified or explained through either standard spiritual doctrine, or scientific method is nearly impossible, even if all my intuition is in fact correct. Such is the life of the mad man, the hermit.

However, there is a power in faith,
or to repeat what Edward Abbey wrote,

"a way of being wrong, which is necessarily a way of being right."

Take the account of Saint Joseph of Copertino during the 17th century. The story starts without Joseph being a Saint, but merely an odd person and most likely a laughable one at that. After all, Joseph claimed he was able to fly. Not like a high jumper, of some wizard of the basketball world, but that he could really fly and float and move about in the ether of air. It started simply: one day he went away from other people, to an obscure corner of the chapel where he was engrossed in prayer. Suddenly he cried out: he had risen up in the air and was flying to a nearby altar. With another cry, he flew back to the corner where he had started his prayers. Joseph was investigated by the Church, acquitted of the charge of practicing deception of false miracles. Against the odds, Joseph soon became a Saint through the accounts and witnesses of "*respectable*" people. Actual observation finally proved he was able to fly. This one example is at least one good proof of the impossible. Not easy to do, but the Catholic Church canonizes only those whom it concludes, beyond doubt, are capable of the acts claimed. I present this not so much as a testament to the power of a God, or the church, but to make clear the possibilities that exist in this richly layered world of ours. Are not unseen things happening all the time? We all know of something we thought impossible to have become possible. We bring Gods back and forth to earth all the time. One person's discovery is another's fantasy.

ii.

Staring straight ahead.   Looking, not seeing.

Gazing and not purposefully thinking.   Weary
of the shape of the clouds and the smell of the breeze, I see a
heron foraging along a narrow sand bar along the Kaw River.

After so much time spent
observing these birds over the past years
I realize that seeing the heron standing, waiting for food by
itself along a river is not really an accurate indication of
the heron in a rookery.

The variety of noise, the clamor, and madness which ensues during
the straightening of the nests, the mating and the feeding of the
young is something which is hard to describe. I believe that to fully
understand the heron it must be seen as part of a more specific
spot on earth. The bird is part of the sycamore tree, part of
the water flowing in a creek, it is partly the color green
filtering throughout the leaves of a valley, part earth deep
between tree roots, part frog, stream water, and partly
the squelch of the red-tailed hawk overhead.
The collection of all these ingredients can
be understood as a sacred spot, fully
realized as the rookery of the great
blues. It is within this realm
that the soul external
is harbored.
There has never been a spot more ripe with an alchemy
of
Place.

Can we learn to worship a creature supported by two thin legs and reaching no more than four-and-a-half feet tall? Can we place at least a part of our understanding of the universe in creatures that have evolved little since the Miocene? Do we dare ignore the accumulation of creative mythology carried forth by previous generations? Can we safely proceed as humans without the feelings of being healed through fear? Can we really be happy without being able to run amuck and ambushed by our need for surprise? In many ways pure rationality and reason are not all that satisfying. This is why we put up with pesky pets, why we like rainstorms, why our favorite days can be cold, windy, and void of sun. I find primordial, deeply hidden and unusual instincts necessary to be satisfied.

105

Surprise is knowledge's victory.

Learning to be fluent or just make sense of the invisible and silence is time consuming. There is no moment when a pause isn't an active gesture. No moment when everything isn't happening. The alchemy of a spot is not so exact as to be four elements equally spread out, but is a mutable thing, swayed from season to season, from water, to fire, to earth, to air—and then of course, there is the fifth element.

This
fifth element
is what emits silence.
The fifth element is spirit and is everything, yet nothing.
Spirit is well-known yet has no recognizable scent.
Its sound is common, yet has never been heard.
It is as clear as seeing the heron for the hundredth time,
and at the same time as fresh as seeing a heron for the

first time.

I suppose it's all really simple then. If in a pouring rainstorm we can stand and take comfort beneath a rookery of heron nests, then for a brief moment all is as wise as a world in creation. All is steeped in primordial fluid, bloody as roots, old as the orders of angels, safe as good thoughts, sharp as

quick scents

.

"Now the angel has come to earth
and the human has arrived
in heaven."

Malcom Godwin.

SWALLOWING
while
OBSERVING

In the end I discover I have given myself to the heron. Observers, without knowing why, will feel a flush of heat over their face, will shake their head and suddenly realize they have become the watched.

This is the twist.
To this reversal there is at once an end
&
a new unexpected
beginning.

I set out merely to discover a place I was told about by a friend, because it sounded like a good adventure for the day. Quickly I became entrenched with fascination and exploration, tied with previous generations. After years of believing I was the one who was doing the watching, the studying and the understanding, I felt my shudder of surprise. At some point, sitting still, watching, I felt a quivering, a gush of heat spill over me,

my heart dropped

as though I were being attacked by surprise. I looked up wondering what had happened and saw the eyes of a great blue heron, no more than twenty yards away, peering directly into me. When we matched eyes, I looked away first. I felt scared, somehow embarrassed. Then a moment more and I felt comforted. I was worthy of being watched, not flown from. I was worthy of interest, at the very least.

This is perhaps an odd place to end the quest,
but I am both exhausted and need to recover from this gaze
upon me.
Never had I expected to become the observed.
I know that all of this thinking about,
watching and trying to understand herons has taken me far,
far away from where I started,
although in just as many ways I now feel I have learned
nothing.
I wonder if now I am about to begin an equally long

reverse *journey* in.

I do know one thing,
which Loren Eiseley has written,

"teachers are not always to be found in school

or in the great laboratory.

Sometimes what we learn depends

upon our own powers of insight."

For now then,
the leaves have fallen off the sycamore trees,
the young herons have learned
to travel and eat on their own.

I straighten out my neck,
tuck my soul into a nearby tree trunk
and let myself rise up in the air,
somewhere between earth

and sky

*

*   *

PRAYERS TO HONOR

THE

GREAT

BLUE HERON

Fire:

sacred

Flame.

We respect

your power and

we present to you the great

blue heron, whom we care for, honor,

love, and respect. Please protect them and

provide them with your good favor. We

trust you to enlighten and enrich them with

your sunlight, to give them needed energy,

strength, and courage. Let the blaze of your

soul bring them growth, and may their

passions be tended with care.

WATER:

Holy water,
we present great blue herons to
you and ask that they never thirst,
that the body of your life sustain them
in every way. Let their flights be

as

flowing

as you, ever

changing, always sacred.
At once rain and evaporation,
then fog, then mist, now river lake
or pond. Soon clouds, tides,
and creek.

EARTH:

Sacred earth, we thank you for your trees,

wood,

leaves.

Honor and respect these

Herons, keeping their bodies strong

and whole. Let no harm come to them.

Let them use your wise medicines when

they encounter sickness. Provide them with

the regenerative powers of growth. know

they use your earth wisely

◆

Air:

Air all around us.
Grant the great blue herons
your quickness when danger is near.
Share your clear eyes for seeing,

your ears for hearing,

your way of discerning. May their breaths

be clean and wholesome.

Let their blood and their wings flow

with your oxygen.

When in your care,

guide them safely

in   flight.

and   migration.

Spirit:

Deeply residing in the middle of all things,
we ask you provide these birds with
gratitude and faith. We know

spirit

is invisible, timeless, thick, and enriched
with the sweet elixir of bliss. Please
Spirit, keep the Heron wedded to
the Earth, the Water, the Air, the Fire.

Notes

Initial numbers for each citation indicate the page within this book where a related quote exists.

Front Matter

7. Nims, John Frederick, ed. "The. XIIII. Booke." Trans. Arthur Golding *Ovid's Metamorphoses: The Arthur Golding Translation*. New York: Macmillan, 1965. P 367-68

11. Leopold, Aldo, Charles Walsh Schwartz, and Aldo Leopold. *A Sand County Almanac. With Other Essays on Conservation from Round River*. New York: Oxford University Press, 1966. P 176

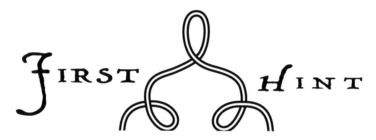

FIRST HINT

15. Holthaus, Gary H., *Skies: Finding a Home in the West*. Tucson: University of Arizona, 1997. P 167

18. Eliade, Mircea, and Willard R. Trask (trans), *The Sacred and the Profane: The Nature of Religion*. Harcourt, Brace, 1959. P 22

20. Nelson, Richard K., *The Island Within*. Vintage, 1991. P 3

22. Eliade, Mircea, and Willard R. Trask (trans), *The Sacred and the Profane: The Nature of Religion*. Harcourt, Brace, 1959. P 12

23. Petersen, Eugene H., *Christ Plays in Ten Thousand Places*. Wm. B. Eerdmans Publishing Co., 2005. P 20

24. Rousseau, Jean-Jacques, Philip Stewart, and Jean Vaché, *Julie, Or, The New Heloise: Letters of Two Lovers Who Live in a Small Town at the Foot of the Alps*. Hanover: Dartmouth College,1997. P 312

25. Merwin, W. S., *"Witness," **The Rain in the Trees: Poems**. New York: Knopf, 1988. P 65

25. Thorpe, Douglas, ***Rapture of the Deep: Reflections on the Wild in Art, Wilderness and the Sacred***. Red Hen, Los Angeles, 2007. P 2

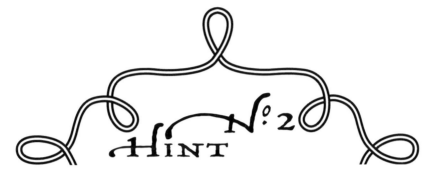

29. Gruchow, Paul, ***Journal of a Prairie Year***, University of Minnesota Press, 1985. P 5

30. Anderson, Sherwood, ***Winesburg, Ohio***, Viking Critical Library, Penquin Books, 1983 ed. P 26

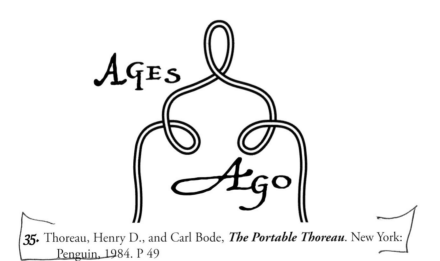

35. Thoreau, Henry D., and Carl Bode, ***The Portable Thoreau***. New York: Penguin, 1984. P 49

37. Nietzsche, Friedrich Wilhelm, Walter Arnold Kaufmann, and R. J. Hollingdale, ***The Will to Power***. Random House, 1967. Aphorism P 419

37. Shepard, Paul, ***Man in the Landscape: A Historic View of the Esthetics of Nature***. University of Georgia, Athens, GA., 2002. P 28

38. Cotnoir, Brian. *"Tabula Smaragdina." **Alchemy***. San Francisco: Samuel Weiser, 2006. P 55-57

39. Camus, Albert, ***The Myth of Sisyphus***, Vintage, 1991 ed. P 20

39. ***Samuel Butler's Notebooks***, E.P. Dutton & Company, 1951. P 283

39. Abbey, Edward, ***Desert Solitaire: A Season in the Wilderness***. Ballantine, 1971. P xi

E**x**PLORING PRE-HISTORIC

54. Von Rad, Gerhard, ***Wisdom in Israel***, SCM Press, London, 1972. P 165

56. Roszak, Theodore, ***The Voice of the Earth***, Simon & Schuster,1992. P 14

57. Gruchow, Paul, ***Journal of a Prairie Year***, Univ. of Minnesota Press,1985. P 5

57. Roszak, Theodore, ***The Voice of the Earth***, Simon & Schuster,1992. P 14

59. E. E. Cummings, ***Poems 1923-1954***, Harcourt Brace, NY, 1954. P 464

60. Watts, Alan, ***The Wisdom of Insecurity***, Vintage Books, 1968. P 24

60. Borges, Jorge Luis, ***The Aleph and other stories***, E.P, Dutton,1978 ed. P 263

The Flavor of Brass

65. Nicholsen, Shierry Weber, *The Love of Nature and the End of the World: The Unspoken Dimensions of Environmental Concern*, MIT Press, 2002. P 156

67. Tsu, Lao, Gia-fu Feng, and Jane English. *"Fourty-one." Tao Te Ching*. New York: Vintage, 1972. N. pag. Print.

71. Merwin, W. S., *"Witness," The Rain in the Trees: Poems*. Knopf, 1988. P 65

71. Faulkner, William, *'The Bear,' The Portable Faulkner*, Penguin Classics, 1977. P 184

73. Abram, David, *The Spell of the Sensuous: Perception and Language in a More-Than-Human World*, Vintage Books, 1996. P 153

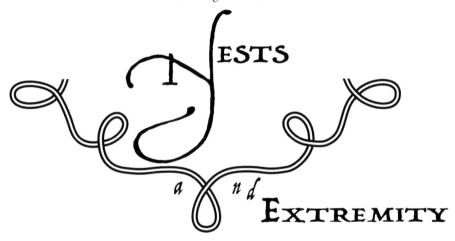

Nests and Extremity

75. Abram, David, *The Spell of the Sensuous: Perception and Language in a More-Than-Human World*, Vintage Books, 1996. P 9

77. Frazer, Sir James George, *"The External Soul in Folk-Tales,"* Chapter LXVI, *The Golden Bough*. MacMillian Company, NY, 1951 ed. P 78

78. Wolf, Robert, *The Triumph of Technique*, Ruskin Press, Halls, Tn. 2003. P 111

Nests and Extremity, CONTINUED

79. Tsu, Lao, Gia-fu Feng, and Jane English. *"Sixty-three." **Tao Te Ching**.* New York: Vintage, 1972. N. pag. Print.

79. Megill, Allen, ***Prophets of Extremity***, University of CA Press, Berkeley, CA, 1987. P 345-346

80. Hocking, William. ***The meaning of God in human experience: a philosophic study of religion***. Yale University Press, 1912. P 484

80. Everson, William, ***The Excesses of God: Robinson Jeffers as a Religious Figure***, Stanford University Press, 1988. P 96

83-84. Frazer, Sir James George, *"The External Soul in Folk-Tales,"* Chapter LX-VI, ***The Golden Bough***. MacMillian Company, 1951, ed. P 776

86. Altizer, Thomas J.J., *"Eternal Recurrence and Kingdom of God,"* ***The New Nietzsche***, ed. David Alison, MIT Press, Cambridge, 1985. P 237

88. Brach, Tara, *"Tara Brach Awakening, Trance of Unworthiness,"* ***Inquiring Mind***, V. 17, No. 2, 2001, http.tarabrach.com/articles/inquiring-traces.html

89. Moore, Thomas, ***"Mystic Clouds and Natural Spirituality,"*** *Orion*, V. 16, No. 3, 1999. P 30-33

90. Gass, William, ***Fiction and the Figures of Life***, David R. Godine Publisher, Boston; 1971. P 9

90. Borges, Jorge Luis, *"Ulrike,"* ***The Book of Sand***, E.P. Dutton Paperback Ed., 1978. P 21

91. Eliade, Mircea, ***Occultism, Witchcraft, and Cultural Fashions: Essays in Comparative Religion***, University of Chicago Press, 1978. P 94

94. Norris, Kathleen, ***The Cloister Walk***, Riverhead Books, 1997. P 11

94. Ware, Bishop Kallistos, ***The Orthodox Way***, St Vladimir's Seminary Press, Crestwood, NY, 1996. P 7

95. Nicholsen, Shierry Weber, ***The Love of Nature and the End of the World: The Unspoken Dimensions of Environmental Concern***, MIT Press, 2002. P 103

HERMITS, Silence & MADNESS

99. Keats, John, *"Keats' letter to Benjamin Bailey, 22 November 1817,"* **Selected Letters**, Oxford University Press, Oxford, 2002. P 36

100. Keats, John, *"Keats' letter to Benjamin Bailey, 22 November 1817,"* **Selected Letters**, Oxford University Press, Oxford, 2002. P 41

101. Snyder, Gary, *"The Etiquette of Freedom,"* **Practice of the Wild**, North Point Press, SF, Ca, 1990. P 12

103. Godwin, Malcolm, **Angels: An Endangered Species**, Simon & Schuster, 1990. P 252

103. Abbey, Edward, **Desert Solitaire: A Season in the Wilderness**. New York: Ballantine, 1971. P xi

SWALLOWING while OBSERVING

109. Godwin, Malcolm, **Angels: An Endangered Species**, Simon & Schuster, 1990. P 249

111. Loren Eiseley, *"The Hidden Teacher,"* **The Star Thrower**, Harvest Book, Harcourt, 1978. P 116

E n d n o t e s

134. Anonymous, ***View of the Markt at 's-Hertogenbosch***, 's-Hertogenbosch c.1530, oil on panel, 126 x 67cm. 's-Hertogenbosch, Noordbrabants Museum.

135. Koldeweij, Jos, Paul Vandenbroeck, and Bernard Vermet. *"The Life and Death of Hieronymus Bosch."* **Hieronymus Bosch: The Complete Paintings and Drawings**. Amsterdam: Ludion Ghent, 2001. 54-55

B I B L I O G R A P H Y

Abbey, Edward. Desert **Solitaire: A Season in the Wilderness**. New York Ballantine, 1983. Print.

Abram, David. **The Spell of the Sensuous: Perception and Language in a More-than-human World**. New York: Pantheon, 1996. Print.

Allen, Hayward. **The Great Blue Heron**. Minocqua, WI: NorthWord,1991. Print.

Anderson, Sherwood, and John H. Ferres. **Sherwood Anderson, Winesburg, Ohio: Text and Criticism**. Harmondsworth: Penguin, 1982. Print.

Borges, Jorge Luis, and Andrew Hurley. **Collected Fictions**. New York, NY, U.S.A.: Viking, 1998. Print.

_____, Jorge Luis, and Eliot Weinberger. **Selected Non-fictions**. New York: Penguin, 2000. Print.

Butler, Robert William. **The Great Blue Heron: A Natural History and Ecology of a Seashore Sentinel**. Vancouver, BC: UBC, 1997. Print.

Crowell, Marnie Reed. **Great Blue: The Odyssey of a Great Blue Heron**. New York: Times, 1980. Print.

Cotnoir, Brian. **Alchemy**. San Francisco.: Samuel Weiser, 2006. Print.

Eiseley, Loren C. **The Firmament of Time**. New York: Atheneum, 1960. Print.

_____, Loren C. **The Star Thrower**. New York: Times, 1978. Print.

Eliade, Mircea, and Willard R. Trask. **The Sacred and the Profane: The Nature of Religion**. New York: Harcourt, Brace, 1959. Print.

BIBLIOGRAPHY, *continued*

Everson, William. *The Excesses of God: Robinson Jeffers as a Religious Figure*. Stanford, CA: Stanford UP, 1988.

Fox, Matthew, and Hildegard. *Illuminations of Hildegard of Bingen*. Santa Fe, NM: Bear &, 1985. Print.

___, Matthew. *Confessions: The Making of a Postdenominational Priest*. San Francisco, CA: Harper San Francisco, 1996. Print.

Frazer, James George. *The Golden Bough; a Study in Magic and Religion*. New York: Macmillan, 1951. Print.

Gibson, Walter S. *Hieronymus Bosch*. London: Thames & Hudson, 1973. Print.

Godwin, Malcolm. *Angels: An Endangered Species*. New York: Simon and Schuster, 1990. Print.

Gruchow, Paul. *Grass Roots: The Universe of Home*. Minneapolis, MN: Milkweed Editions, 1995. Print.

Hocking, William. *The meaning of God in human experience: a philosophic study of religion*. Yale University Press, 1912. Print.

Holthaus, Gary H. *Wide Skies: Finding a Home in the West*. Tucson: University of Arizona, 1997. Print.

Jensen, Derrick. *A Language Older than Words*. New York: Context, 2000. Print.

Kallistos. *The Orthodox Way*. Crestwood, NY: St. Vladimir's Seminary, 1995. Print.

Koldeweij, Jos, Paul Vandenbroeck, and Bernard Vermet. *Hieronymus Bosch: The Complete Paintings and Drawings*. Amsterdam: Ludion Ghent, 2001. Print.

Lane, Belden C. *Landscapes of the Sacred: Geography and Narrative in American Spirituality*. Baltimore, MD: Johns Hopkins UP, 2002. Print.

____, Belden C. *The Solace of Fierce Landscapes: Exploring Desert and Mountain Spirituality*. New York: Oxford UP, 1998. Print.

Leopold, Aldo, Charles Walsh Schwartz, and Aldo Leopold. *A Sand County Almanac. With Other Essays on Conservation from Round River*. New York: Oxford UP, 1966. Print.

BIBLIOGRAPHY, *continued*

Lopez, Barry Holstun. *Of Wolves and Men*. New York: Scribner, 1978. Print.

Maitland, Sara. *A Joyful Theology: Creation, Commitment, and an Awesome God*. Minneapolis, MN: Augsburg, 2002. Print.

Megill, Allan. *Prophets of Extremity: Nietzsche, Heidegger, Foucault, Derrida*. Berkeley: University of California, 1985. Print.

Merwin, W. S. *The Rain in the Trees: Poems*. New York: Knopf, 1988. Print.

Napora, Joe. *Flight of the Heron*. N.p.: Bullhead; First Edition, 1996. Print.

Nelson, Richard K. *The Island Within*. New York: Vintage, 1991. Print.

Nicholsen, Shierry Weber. *The Love of Nature and the End of the World: The Unspoken Dimensions of Environmental Concern*. Cambridge, MA: MIT, 2002. Print.

Nietzsche, Friedrich Wilhelm, Walter Arnold. Kaufmann, and R. J. Hollingdale *The Will to Power*. New York: Vintage, 1968. Print.

Norris, Kathleen. *The Cloister Walk*. New York: Riverhead, 1997. Print.

Ovid. *Ovid's Metamorphoses: The Arthur Golding Translation, 1567*. Trans. Arthur Golding. Ed. John Frederick Nims. New York: Macmillan, 1965. Print.

Roszak, Theodore. *The Voice of the Earth*. New York: Simon & Schuster, 1992 Print.

Schumacher, E. F. *A Guide for the Perplexed*. New York: Harper & Row, 1977 Print.

Semken, S. H. *Moving with the Elements*. North Liberty, IA: Ice Cube, 1998. Print.

_____, S. H. *The Tin Prayer: Words of the Wolverine: Words from the Wild Testament*. North Liberty, IA: Ice Cube, 2001. Print.

Shepard, Paul. *Man in the Landscape: A Historic View of the Esthetics of Nature*. New York: Knopf, 1967. Print.

BIBLIOGRAPHY, *continued*

Snyder, Gary. *The Practice of the Wild: Essays*. San Francisco: North Point, 1990. Print.

Telford, John, and Terry Tempest. Williams. *Coyote's Canyon*. Salt Lake City: Peregrine Smith, 1989. Print.

Thorpe, Douglas. *Rapture of the Deep: Reflections on the Wild in Art, Wilderness and the Sacred*. Los Angeles: Red Hen, 2007. Print.

Tsu, Lao. *Tao Te Ching*. Trans. Jane English and Gia-fu Feng. New York: Vintage, 1972. Print.

Wolf, Robert. *The Triumph of Technique: The Industrialization of Agriculture and the Destruction of Rural America*. Halls, TN: Ruskin, 2003. Print.

ILLUSTRATIONS

Initial numbers indicate the location of a drawing in its complete form within this book, while any subsequent number(s) pertain to details of that same image also having a different placement. Drawn images utilized for the interior of this publication were produced between 2004-05. All four of these drawings have since been modified.

Cover, 31, 66, 101. Andrew R. Driscoll, *Mocha Dick*, mixed materials on laid paper, 270.40 x 431.80mm., 2009-10

63, 48. Andrew R. Driscoll, *Origin Tree*, mixed materials on laid paper, 2013

96, 69. Andrew R. Driscoll, *Squaring of the Nest*, mixed materials on laid paper, 2013-14

113, 19. Andrew R. Driscoll, *Heron Offering*, mixed materials on laid paper, 2013

122, 20, 27. Andrew R. Driscoll, *Ardea herodias*, mixed materials on laid paper, 2013-14

please see * for further details

A REVERSE JOURNEY IN

Although in different form and content this project has its origins in the book *The Great Blues*. Yet despite being published in 2005 the memories encapsulated in *The Great Blues* remained a recurring subject of renewed conversation between Steve and Andrew. Such collective times, beyond endless excursions across the Great Plains, included seven (7) years when Andrew worked for John Talleur, University of Kanasas Professor of Printmaking, as the studio assistant in John's

THE HOLISEVENTH PRESS.

Unexpectedly, and many years removed, an impression from a winter view outside the Driscoll's 2012 residence in Cham, Switzerland, combined to produce a look backward.

An oblique connection came pouring out from a source utilized for visual interpretation of the story within the previously noted blue heron book. Contained within it exists a description and painted image of Heironymus Bosch's home following his marriage. The painting presented elements strikingly reminiscent of the church of St. James amid a Swiss wintertime, while accompanying the painting (circa 1530) is a description of Bosch residing at "...the SEVENTH house from the right." John Talleur, one keen to play off puns as well as visual cues (admittedly, one such presently related cue has been artificially & shamefully  heightened), would have instantaneously seen the parallels as he had even further produced within his own business cards:

THE HOLISEVENTH PRESS

hand printed illustrated books

242 Concord road, Lawrence, KS 66044   913 843 6819

Ample impetus provided. Our earlier heron-based efforts were to be reborn.

———————

Andrew R. Driscoll received a Masters of Fine Arts in Painting from The School of the Art Institute of Chicago. Among other occupations, he has taught art and art history at the collegiate level for over twelve years. Andrew is a practicing painter and draftsman having an invested kinship with the 18th and 19th century Romantic Movement's creative processes as reflected through nature. His paintings, prints, and drawings exist in national and international collections.

Steve Semken remains fascinated by the habits of great blue herons. He is an award-winning author of several books including ***Moving With The Elements*** and ***The Tin Prayer***. He has been the Writer-in-Residence at the Island Institute in Sitka, Alaska, as well as speaker, and teacher, at workshops on writing and publishing all over the United States. In 1993 he founded the Ice Cube Press, which is dedicated to relentlessly promoting a better understanding of the merits inherently found within the Midwest through the literary arts.

A SUBSTANTIAL SUBSTRATE

Each original drawn image within this book exists upon handmade laid paper produced by the firm J. B. Green in England. The paper bears unique watermarks—Christ's head within St. Veronica's veil above the date 1399; an upraised hand, palm forward, having a quatrefoil atop the middle finger; the monogram of FJH, who was the initial creator of the moulds used for the paper's production. These sheets, each with the dimensions of 393.70 x 520.70mm., belonged to John Talleur. They were provided to Andrew as partial payment for work he performed at the

THE HOLISEVENTH PRESS.

GARAMOND
The text has ben set in Adobe Garamond. The garamond typeface was designed by Jean Jannon in 1615. Garamond is characterized by little contrast between the thick and thin letter strokes, heavily bracketed serifs and oblique stress. The letterforms are open and round, making the face extremely readable.

OPERINA

Operina is a type font based on a 16th-century lettering model of the
scribe Vicentino Ludovico degli Arrighi
used in his 1522 instructional lettering book,
"La Operina da Imparare di scrivere littera Cancellarescha."
This book contains what is considered to be the earliest printed
examples of Chancery Cursive.
The digitally modified versions utilized for this present
publication were produced
by James Grieshaber.

137

The Ice Cube Press began publishing in 1993
to focus on how to live with the natural world and to better
understand how people can best live together in the commu-
nities they share and inhabit. Using the literary arts to explore
life and experiences in the heartland of the United States we
have been recognized by a number of well-known writers
including: Gary Snyder, Gene Logsdon, Wes Jackson,
Patricia Hampl, Greg Brown, Jim Harrison, Annie Dillard,
Ken Burns, Roz Chast, Daniel Menaker, Jane Hamilton,
Kathleen Norris, Janisse Ray, Craig Lesley, Alison Deming,
Richard Rhodes, Michael Pollan, and Barry Lopez. We've
published a number of well-known authors including:
Elizabeth McCracken, Mary Swander, Jim Heynen, Mary
Pipher, Bill Holm, Connie Mutel, John T. Price, Carol Bly,
Marvin Bell, Debra Marquart, Ted Kooser, Dean
Bakopoulos, Stephanie Mills, Bill McKibben, Craig Lesley,
and Paul Gruchow. We have won several publishing awards
over the last twenty-plus years. Check out our books at our
web site, join our facebook group, follow us on twitter, visit
booksellers, museum shops, or any place you can find good
books and discover why we continue striving to,
"hear the other side."

Ice Cube Press, LLC (est. 1993)
205 N. Front Street
North Liberty, Iowa 52317-9302
steve@icecubepress.com
twitter @icecubepress
www.icecubepress.com

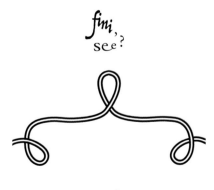

139

safeguard –
Mother Earth

"T"

Blue   @   (sculpture)

Heron

                         @

          1st year @

     Cabin – Hayward

                    Wisc .

2 Days at
Kinnamon
    School

on "Rez"
@ Anishinaba

(Pow Wow)

July
2011

LCO

Lac-Courte –
– Oreilles

(Chippewa)

"Anishina beg" people of
        Odaawaa-Zaaga'–
              – iganiing